85 Remarkable Women in History

Gabriella Goldberger

Published by Azure Time Press, 2023.

85 REMARKABLE WOMEN IN HISTORY

First edition. September 20, 2023.

ISBN: 979-8223693918

Written by Gabriella Goldberger.

Table of Contents

To the fearless women who dared to dream, defied expectations, and illuminated the path for others to follow. May their stories serve as eternal beacons of possibility for each of us.

Chapter 1: Pioneering Women in Science

Barbara McClintock: Unraveling the Secrets of Jumping Genes

In the annals of science, the name Barbara McClintock stands as a testament to the power of perseverance, curiosity, and groundbreaking discovery. Born in 1902 in Hartford, Connecticut, Barbara McClintock's journey through the world of genetics would forever alter our understanding of the genetic code, unlocking the mysteries of transposons, the enigmatic "jumping genes."

From her early days on a farm, McClintock's affinity for the natural world was unmistakable. Her inquisitive mind thirsted for knowledge, a desire that would drive her to challenge the gender norms of her time. In an era when women in science were often met with closed doors, McClintock pushed forward. She pursued her studies at Cornell University, earning a Ph.D. in Botany in 1927.

It was her deep fascination with maize genetics that laid the foundation for her groundbreaking work. McClintock's choice of maize as her research subject may have seemed unremarkable at first glance, but it was here, within the unassuming cornfields, that she would uncover the extraordinary.

In the 1940s, McClintock embarked on a series of meticulous experiments that would forever change the course of genetics. As she peered into the intricate world of maize chromosomes, she began to notice something peculiar—genetic elements that seemed to defy the rules. These elements, as she discovered, had the astonishing ability to move within the genome, jumping from one location to another. She aptly coined them "transposons" or "jumping genes."

The scientific community initially met McClintock's findings with skepticism and resistance. The concept of mobile genetic elements challenging the stability of the genetic code was nothing short of revolutionary. But McClintock was undeterred. Her tenacity in the face of adversity drove her to accumulate a mountain of evidence, gradually compelling her peers to recognize the importance of her discoveries.

Her groundbreaking work did more than just challenge the status quo—it transformed our understanding of genetics. McClintock's research illuminated the dynamic nature of genomes, emphasizing that genes were not fixed entities but could actively reshuffle and reconfigure themselves. Transposons, it turned out, played a pivotal role in genetic variation and adaptation, impacting the evolution of species.

In 1983, Barbara McClintock was awarded the Nobel Prize in Physiology or Medicine, an acknowledgment of her extraordinary contributions to science. Her journey from a determined young woman with a passion for genetics to a groundbreaking scientist who unraveled the secrets of jumping genes serves as a powerful inspiration.

Beyond the accolades and recognition, McClintock's legacy endures as a beacon of scientific curiosity and resilience. Her work fundamentally altered our perception of the genetic code and continues to shape the field of genetics to this day. Barbara McClintock's story is not just a chapter in the history of science; it is a testament to the boundless possibilities of human inquiry and the enduring impact of those who dare to challenge the unknown.

Dorothy Crowfoot Hodgkin: Unveiling Molecular Mysteries through X-ray Crystallography

Dorothy Crowfoot Hodgkin, a luminary in the world of science, left an indelible mark on the field of chemistry through her pioneering work in X-ray crystallography. Born in Cairo, Egypt, in 1910, Hodgkin's journey through the intricate world of molecular structures would revolutionize our understanding of life at its most fundamental level.

Hodgkin's early years were marked by academic excellence and a keen interest in the sciences. Her academic pursuits eventually led her to Oxford University, where she immersed herself in the world of chemistry. It was during this time that she encountered X-ray crystallography, a groundbreaking technique that would become her lifelong passion.

In an era where opportunities for women in science were limited, Hodgkin's unwavering determination propelled her forward. She ventured into uncharted territory, applying X-ray crystallography to unveil the mysteries of molecular structures. Her pioneering spirit led her to unravel the intricate arrangements of atoms within crystals, a task that required meticulous precision and patience.

One of Hodgkin's most significant achievements was determining the structure of penicillin, the groundbreaking antibiotic that had revolutionized medicine. Her work not only confirmed the molecular structure of penicillin but also showcased the power of X-ray crystallography in elucidating complex molecular arrangements.

But Hodgkin's contributions extended far beyond antibiotics. Her remarkable work also led to the elucidation of the structure of insulin, a hormone critical in regulating blood sugar levels. This breakthrough provided invaluable insights into diabetes and paved the way for advances in the treatment of the disease.

In 1964, Dorothy Crowfoot Hodgkin's dedication and groundbreaking contributions were duly recognized when she was awarded the Nobel Prize in Chemistry. Her receipt of this prestigious honor marked a watershed moment not only for her but for the field of crystallography as a whole. She became the third woman to receive the Nobel Prize in Chemistry, a testament to her extraordinary achievements and the barriers she had broken.

Hodgkin's work was nothing short of transformative. Her innovative use of X-ray crystallography shattered the barriers of the unknown, revealing the intricacies of molecular structures in unprecedented detail. Her tireless efforts broadened our understanding of life's building blocks and laid the foundation for advancements in chemistry, biology, and medicine.

Beyond her scientific prowess, Dorothy Crowfoot Hodgkin's legacy endures as an inspiration to women in science and to aspiring scientists everywhere. Her unyielding dedication to unraveling the mysteries of the molecular world serves as a reminder that the pursuit of knowledge knows no boundaries.

As we celebrate the life and work of Dorothy Crowfoot Hodgkin, we honor not only her groundbreaking discoveries but also her enduring spirit of inquiry and her lasting impact on the scientific community. Her legacy continues to illuminate the path forward for future generations of scientists and explorers, reminding us of the profound beauty and complexity of the natural world.

Marie Curie: Discovering Radioactivity

Marie Curie, born Maria Skłodowska in Warsaw, Poland, in 1867, was destined to become one of the most influential figures in the history of science. Her journey from a young woman with a thirst for knowledge in a society that often limited women's access to higher education to a groundbreaking scientist who revolutionized our understanding of the atom and radiation serves as a testament to her unwavering dedication, intelligence, and determination.

Marie's early years were marked by academic excellence, and she hungered for the kind of education that was often denied to women in the late 19th century. In 1891, she left her native Poland and ventured to Paris, a city renowned for its intellectual vibrancy, to pursue a degree in physics and mathematics at the Sorbonne. This decision marked the beginning of her transformative journey.

While studying in Paris, Marie met Pierre Curie, a fellow scientist, and the two quickly fell in love. They shared not only a deep affection for each other but also a passion for scientific inquiry. Their partnership was characterized by mutual respect and a shared commitment to advancing human understanding.

The Curies' groundbreaking work in the nascent field of radioactivity soon became the focus of their scientific pursuits. Their pioneering research led to the discovery of two new elements: polonium, named after Marie's homeland, and radium, which emitted an astonishing level of radioactivity. These discoveries were groundbreaking, and the term "radioactivity" itself was coined by Marie Curie to describe the phenomenon they observed.

One of the remarkable aspects of Marie's work was her unrelenting dedication to her laboratory experiments. She and Pierre often worked tirelessly with minimal protective measures, exposed to radioactive materials that posed significant health risks. Their pursuit of knowledge was not without personal sacrifice, as both of them would later experience health issues related to their work.

In 1903, Marie Curie made history by becoming the first woman to be awarded a Nobel Prize. She shared the Nobel Prize in Physics with Pierre and another scientist, Henri Becquerel, in recognition of their groundbreaking research on radioactivity. Eight years later, in 1911, Marie received her second Nobel Prize, this time in Chemistry, for her discovery of radium and polonium and her thorough investigations into their properties.

Marie Curie's scientific achievements had profound implications, not only for the field of physics and chemistry but also for medicine. Radium's unique properties made it a powerful tool in the treatment of cancer. During World War I, Marie's commitment to science and humanity led her to establish mobile radiography units, providing vital medical support to wounded soldiers.

Tragically, Pierre Curie's life was cut short in 1906 when he died in a street accident. Despite this devastating loss, Marie continued her scientific pursuits, becoming the first female professor at the Sorbonne and dedicating herself to educating future generations of scientists.

Marie Curie's legacy endures as an inspiration to scientists worldwide, especially women. Her life story serves as a powerful reminder of the boundless potential of human curiosity, determination, and resilience in the face of adversity. As we celebrate her remarkable achievements, we honor not only her groundbreaking discoveries but also her indomitable spirit that continues to inspire generations of scientists to push the boundaries of knowledge.

Marie Curie's legacy is not just a story of scientific achievement; it is a testament to the profound impact one individual can have on the world when driven by an unwavering commitment to uncover the secrets of the universe.

Marie Curie's remarkable journey from an aspiring student to a pioneering scientist was marked by numerous challenges, sacrifices, and groundbreaking discoveries. Her dedication to the pursuit of knowledge and her relentless curiosity propelled her into the annals of scientific history.

After the untimely death of Pierre Curie in 1906, Marie faced the daunting task of carrying on their research and legacy. Despite the emotional and professional setbacks, she remained resolute in her commitment to science. In 1914, she became the director of the Radium Institute in Paris, a position that allowed her to further her research and mentor future scientists.

Marie's work with radium and radioactivity continued to evolve, and she made significant contributions to the understanding of the behavior of radioactive elements. Her groundbreaking experiments paved the way for future advancements in nuclear physics and chemistry. She also played a crucial role in the development of X-ray technology for medical applications during World War I, earning her the nickname "the Angel of the Battlefield."

In addition to her scientific endeavors, Marie Curie was a passionate advocate for the use of radium in medical treatments. She traveled extensively to raise funds for research and medical applications, making it her mission to ensure that the benefits of radium were accessible to the wider world. Her tireless efforts led to the establishment of radium therapy centers and research facilities across the globe.

Despite her numerous accomplishments, Marie faced significant challenges as a woman in a male-dominated scientific world. She often struggled for recognition and faced criticism and skepticism from some quarters. However, her dedication and the undeniable significance of her work gradually earned her the respect and admiration of the scientific community.

Marie Curie's life was not solely defined by her scientific achievements; it was also marked by personal tragedy and sacrifice. Her exposure to radioactive materials during her research ultimately took a toll on her health. In her later years, she battled severe health issues, including aplastic anemia, which was likely a result of her prolonged exposure to radiation.

Tragically, on July 4, 1934, Marie Curie passed away at the age of 66, leaving behind a legacy that continues to shape the world of science and inspire generations of scientists, especially women. Her contributions to our understanding of radioactivity and her unwavering commitment to the betterment of humanity through scientific research remain unparalleled.

Marie Curie's life story is a testament to the power of perseverance, intellect, and determination. Her indomitable spirit and passion for knowledge continue to serve as an enduring source of inspiration to scientists and thinkers around the world. As we reflect on her remarkable journey, we are reminded of the profound impact that one individual, driven by an insatiable curiosity and a thirst for discovery, can have on the advancement of human knowledge and the betterment of society.

In celebrating Marie Curie's life and legacy, we honor not only her scientific achievements but also her unwavering commitment to the pursuit of truth, the advancement of science, and the alleviation of human suffering. Her story is a beacon of hope and a reminder that, with determination and dedication, individuals can transcend societal constraints and make lasting contributions to the world. Marie Curie's legacy continues to illuminate the path forward for future generations of scientists and explorers.

In the midst of her groundbreaking research, Marie Curie's tireless dedication to her work and her insatiable curiosity led her to make profound discoveries that fundamentally altered the course of scientific history. One of her most remarkable achievements was the isolation of pure radium, a feat that showcased her exceptional skills as a chemist and solidified her reputation as a scientific luminary.

Radium, one of the radioactive elements Marie had discovered alongside her husband Pierre, proved to be an elusive and challenging substance to isolate. It was embedded in complex ores, making the extraction process both intricate and hazardous. Yet, Marie was undeterred by the challenges and complexities of this task.

She developed innovative methods to separate radium from other materials, demonstrating her mastery of analytical chemistry. Through meticulous and painstaking work, Marie managed to isolate tiny quantities of pure radium, which she presented to the world in 1910. This achievement marked a turning point not only in the history of science but also in the field of medicine.

The discovery of pure radium opened up new possibilities for medical applications. Radium's intense radioactivity made it a valuable tool in the treatment of cancer, particularly in the form of radium therapy. Marie's groundbreaking work laid the foundation for the development of radiation therapy in oncology, offering a ray of hope to countless patients suffering from malignant tumors.

Marie Curie's dedication to the beneficial applications of her research was exemplified during World War I when she directed her efforts toward supporting the war effort. She recognized the potential of radiography in the medical field, especially in diagnosing and treating injuries on the battlefield. With her characteristic determination, she spearheaded the creation of mobile radiography units, known as "Little Curies," that provided crucial medical care to wounded soldiers.

The impact of Marie Curie's pioneering research on radium extended far beyond the laboratory. Her work not only advanced the fields of science and medicine but also transformed the way society viewed the potential of scientific discovery. Marie was acutely aware of the profound responsibility that came with her groundbreaking research. She saw the potential for both tremendous good and potential harm in the use of radioactive materials. Her dedication to the safe and responsible use of radium in medical treatments underscored her commitment to the betterment of humanity.

Marie Curie's enduring legacy as a scientist and humanitarian continues to inspire generations of researchers and healthcare professionals. Her relentless pursuit of knowledge, her fearless exploration of the unknown, and her unwavering commitment to the well-being of others serve as a powerful testament to the impact one individual can have on the world.

As we reflect on her remarkable achievements, we celebrate not only her scientific brilliance but also her remarkable resilience, determination, and the boundless possibilities that lie within the realm of human discovery. Marie Curie's life story is a testament to the transformative power of scientific exploration and the enduring legacy that can be forged through a commitment to improving the human condition.

Jane Goodall: Transforming our Understanding of Primates

In the lush, untamed wilderness of Gombe Stream National Park in Tanzania, a young woman named Jane Goodall embarked on an extraordinary journey that would forever change the way we perceive and understand our closest relatives in the animal kingdom. Jane's groundbreaking work with chimpanzees not only redefined the field of primatology but also reshaped our concept of human-animal relationships and the boundaries of scientific exploration.

Born on April 3, 1934, in London, England, Jane's childhood fascination with animals and her insatiable curiosity about the natural world foreshadowed the remarkable path she would follow. Despite lacking formal scientific training, her innate connection with animals and her determination led her to the shores of Lake Tanganyika in 1960, where she began her groundbreaking research on wild chimpanzees.

Jane's approach to studying primates was unconventional at the time. Instead of observing chimpanzees from a distance, she immersed herself in their world, spending hours upon hours in close proximity to these enigmatic creatures. Her patient and unobtrusive methods allowed her to gain the trust of the chimpanzees and observe their behavior in an unprecedented manner.

One of Jane's most significant discoveries was the recognition that chimpanzees, like humans, possess a rich and complex social structure. She observed them forming close-knit family units, nurturing their young, and displaying a wide range of emotions, including joy, sorrow, and even aggression. Her observations shattered the long-held belief that only humans had the capacity for such behaviors.

In 1960, Jane made a groundbreaking observation that would forever alter our understanding of chimpanzees: she witnessed a chimpanzee named David Greybeard using a blade of grass as a tool to extract termites from their mound. This discovery challenged the prevailing notion that tool use was a uniquely human trait. Jane's findings demonstrated that chimpanzees had the cognitive ability to fashion and use tools, a revelation that had profound implications for the field of primatology and our understanding of the evolutionary history of our species.

Jane's pioneering work not only revolutionized our understanding of chimpanzees but also highlighted the urgent need for conservation efforts to protect these remarkable animals and their habitats. She became a passionate advocate for wildlife conservation and the preservation of natural ecosystems.

In 1977, Jane Goodall established the Jane Goodall Institute, dedicated to the conservation of chimpanzees and their habitats, as well as to the promotion of environmental education and sustainable practices. Her tireless efforts in raising awareness about the plight of chimpanzees and other endangered species earned her recognition as a leading voice in the global conservation movement.

Over the decades, Jane's work has inspired countless individuals to pursue careers in primatology, conservation, and environmental science. Her commitment to scientific rigor, compassion for animals, and dedication to conservation serve as a model for aspiring scientists and advocates worldwide.

As we reflect on the life and work of Jane Goodall, we are reminded of the transformative power of curiosity, empathy, and a deep connection to the natural world. Her pioneering research not only expanded our knowledge of primates but also deepened our appreciation for the interconnectedness of all life on Earth. Jane Goodall's legacy continues to inspire generations of scientists, conservationists, and nature enthusiasts to explore, protect, and cherish our planet and its diverse inhabitants.

Jane Goodall's groundbreaking research with chimpanzees not only redefined our understanding of these intelligent and social animals but also had profound implications for the broader fields of primatology, anthropology, and environmental conservation. Her work went beyond scientific observation; it underscored the importance of empathy, ethical treatment of animals, and the interconnectedness of all life on Earth.

Jane's commitment to her research in Gombe Stream National Park was unwavering. She meticulously documented the behaviors, social interactions, and individual personalities of the chimpanzees she studied. Her observations challenged existing paradigms and revealed the striking similarities between humans and chimpanzees in terms of emotions, social bonds, and even the capacity for aggression.

One of the most significant aspects of Jane's work was her focus on individual chimpanzees and her practice of giving them names rather than numbers. This personal approach not only emphasized the uniqueness of each chimpanzee but also fostered a sense of connection and empathy between the researcher and her subjects. It was an early acknowledgment of the moral and ethical considerations inherent in scientific research involving animals.

In addition to her pioneering research, Jane Goodall became a tireless advocate for the ethical treatment of animals. She spoke out against the use of chimpanzees in medical experiments and the pet trade, advocating for their rights and well-being. Her efforts led to greater awareness and changes in public perception, as well as policy changes aimed at protecting chimpanzees and other animals from exploitation.

Throughout her career, Jane's work extended beyond the boundaries of traditional scientific research. She recognized the importance of engaging the public and educating future generations about the wonders of the natural world. Her book, "In the Shadow of Man," and the subsequent documentary film, "Miss Goodall and the Wild Chimpanzees," brought her work to a global audience and inspired countless individuals to become stewards of the environment.

In 1986, Jane Goodall founded the Roots & Shoots program, a global youth-led environmental and humanitarian initiative that empowers young people to take action on issues they care about. This program has since engaged millions of young people in projects aimed at promoting conservation, sustainability, and social responsibility.

Jane's contributions to science, conservation, and education earned her numerous awards and accolades, including the Kyoto Prize, the Benjamin Franklin Medal in Life Science, and the Templeton Prize. She was appointed a United Nations Messenger of Peace in 2002, further amplifying her impact on global conservation efforts.

As we reflect on Jane Goodall's legacy, we are reminded of the transformative power of scientific inquiry driven by compassion, empathy, and a deep sense of responsibility for the natural world. Her work transcends the boundaries of science and resonates with the fundamental human values of empathy and stewardship of the Earth.

Jane Goodall's pioneering research not only expanded our understanding of primates but also catalyzed a global movement for conservation and ethical treatment of animals. Her life's work serves as an enduring source of inspiration, reminding us of our shared responsibility to protect the fragile ecosystems of our planet and the diverse species that call it home.

In celebrating Jane Goodall's contributions to science and conservation, we honor not only her scientific achievements but also her enduring commitment to creating a more compassionate and sustainable world for all living beings.

Rosalind Franklin: Contributing to the DNA Double Helix Discovery

In the mid-20th century, amidst the fervor of scientific exploration and discovery, Rosalind Franklin emerged as a brilliant and tenacious researcher whose contributions to the field of molecular biology played a critical role in unraveling one of the greatest mysteries of life: the structure of DNA. Rosalind's pioneering work in X-ray crystallography laid the foundation for understanding the iconic double helix structure of DNA and paved the way for groundbreaking breakthroughs in genetics and molecular biology.

Born in London in 1920, Rosalind Franklin displayed an early aptitude for science and mathematics. Her academic journey took her to Newnham College, Cambridge, where she excelled in physical chemistry. Her fascination with the mysteries of the physical world, coupled with her exceptional analytical skills, soon led her to the burgeoning field of X-ray crystallography.

Rosalind's entry into the field of crystallography marked the beginning of a scientific journey that would ultimately shape the course of molecular biology. In 1951, she joined King's College London as a research fellow and began her work on the structure of DNA.

At King's College, Rosalind focused her efforts on studying DNA fibers using X-ray crystallography, a technique that involved directing X-rays at crystalline structures to create diffraction patterns. These patterns, when analyzed, could reveal the three-dimensional arrangement of atoms within a crystal. Rosalind's meticulous approach and keen attention to detail were key to her success in this complex and challenging field.

One of Rosalind Franklin's most significant contributions was the famous Photo 51, an X-ray diffraction image of a DNA fiber. This image, captured in 1952, provided crucial insights into the structure of DNA. It revealed a distinctive X-shaped pattern that hinted at a helical structure, marking a critical breakthrough in the quest to understand DNA's architecture.

The Photo 51 image was, in fact, a key piece of evidence that contributed to the elucidation of the DNA double helix. James Watson and Francis Crick, two scientists working at the University of Cambridge, were able to build a physical model of the DNA molecule based on Rosalind's X-ray data and additional insights from her research. In 1953, Watson and Crick published their groundbreaking paper describing the double helical structure of DNA.

While Watson and Crick received widespread recognition for their discovery, it is important to acknowledge Rosalind Franklin's pivotal role in providing essential data and insights. Her meticulous work with X-ray crystallography laid the foundation for their breakthrough. Additionally, her research extended beyond DNA to include studies of other important biomolecules, such as RNA and viruses.

Tragically, Rosalind Franklin's contributions to science were cut short when she passed away from ovarian cancer in 1958 at the age of 37. Her untimely death marked a profound loss to the scientific community, but her legacy endured.

In the years following her death, recognition of Rosalind Franklin's contributions grew, and her pivotal role in the DNA discovery became more widely acknowledged. Today, she is celebrated as a trailblazer in the fields of molecular biology and X-ray crystallography.

Rosalind Franklin's life and work serve as a testament to the power of perseverance, intellectual rigor, and dedication to scientific inquiry. Her groundbreaking research on the structure of DNA not only reshaped our understanding of genetics but also laid the foundation for advancements in fields ranging from biotechnology to medicine.

As we commemorate Rosalind Franklin's remarkable contributions, we are reminded of the countless unsung heroes in the scientific community whose dedication and intellect continue to drive human progress and expand the boundaries of knowledge.

Rachel Carson: Launching the Modern Environmental Movement

In the tranquil surroundings of the Maine coast, Rachel Carson found inspiration for her lifelong mission—to raise awareness about the fragile balance of nature and the perils of environmental degradation. With her seminal work, "Silent Spring," published in 1962, Rachel not only sounded an alarm about the harmful effects of pesticides but also ignited the modern environmental movement, transforming the way we view our planet and our responsibility to protect it.

Rachel Louise Carson was born in Springdale, Pennsylvania, in 1907. Her childhood was marked by a deep connection to nature, nurtured by family outings and a love for the outdoors. This early affinity for the natural world laid the foundation for her future career as a biologist and writer.

Carson's academic journey led her to pursue a master's degree in zoology from Johns Hopkins University, where she honed her skills as a writer and scientist. She initially worked as a marine biologist with the U.S. Bureau of Fisheries, a role that allowed her to explore the marine ecosystems of the Atlantic Ocean and Gulf of Mexico.

Her passion for the oceans and marine life became evident in her first three books, which were written with both scientific rigor and a lyrical style. Her books, including "Under the Sea-Wind" and "The Sea Around Us," received critical acclaim and established her as a prominent nature writer in the 1950s.

However, it was "Silent Spring," published in 1962, that catapulted Rachel Carson into the role of a pioneering environmentalist. The book was a meticulously researched exposé on the detrimental effects of synthetic pesticides, particularly DDT, on the environment, wildlife, and human health. It was a wake-up call to the world about the unintended consequences of modern industrial practices.

"Silent Spring" took its title from the eerie phenomenon Carson described—the absence of birdsong in areas where pesticides had been heavily used, indicating a decline in bird populations. Carson's compelling narrative and passionate advocacy for the environment struck a chord with readers, inspiring widespread concern and calls for action.

The book's impact was profound. It led to increased public awareness about the dangers of pesticides and sparked a wave of environmental activism. Carson's eloquent and scientifically grounded writing compelled governments to reevaluate their pesticide policies. In 1963, spurred by the public outcry generated by "Silent Spring," President John F. Kennedy's Science Advisory Committee conducted an inquiry into the safety and regulation of pesticides, ultimately leading to the banning of DDT in the United States.

Rachel Carson's work not only exposed the threats posed by pesticides but also emphasized the interconnectedness of all living organisms and ecosystems. She articulated the concept of the "web of life," where each species, no matter how seemingly insignificant, played a crucial role in maintaining the balance of nature.

Tragically, Rachel Carson's advocacy came at a personal cost. She faced fierce opposition and criticism from the chemical industry and proponents of pesticide use, who sought to discredit her work. Despite the challenges and backlash, she remained steadfast in her commitment to raising environmental consciousness.

Rachel Carson's legacy extends far beyond "Silent Spring." Her work laid the foundation for modern environmentalism, influencing the establishment of the

U.S. Environmental Protection Agency (EPA) and the passage of landmark environmental laws such as the Clean Air Act and the Clean Water Act.

Carson's writings, which combined scientific insight with a profound love for nature, continue to inspire generations of environmentalists, conservationists, and scientists. Her message is a reminder that our actions have consequences for the natural world, and it is our collective responsibility to safeguard the planet for future generations.

As we reflect on Rachel Carson's enduring impact, we are reminded of the power of words and science to effect change. Her legacy serves as a beacon of hope, urging us to revere the beauty of the natural world, protect its delicate balance, and strive for a more harmonious relationship with the environment.

Chapter 2: Visionary Women in Literature

Audre Lorde: A Beacon of Intersectional Feminism and Social Justice

Audre Lorde, a luminary in the realms of literature, poetry, and civil rights activism, left an enduring legacy that transcends generations. Born in New York City in 1934, her life's work was dedicated to challenging societal norms, amplifying marginalized voices, and advocating for justice on multiple fronts.

From an early age, Lorde exhibited an unquenchable thirst for knowledge and a talent for expression. Her journey through the world of literature and activism began with an appreciation for the written word and a commitment to using it as a tool for change.

Lorde's literary prowess shone brightly in her powerful writings, which delved deep into the interconnected issues of race, gender, and sexuality. Her words were both a mirror reflecting the struggles of marginalized communities and a rallying cry for social justice. With unparalleled eloquence and insight, she confronted the injustices that plagued society, challenging the status quo with unwavering determination.

One of Audre Lorde's most significant contributions to the world of literature and advocacy was her unwavering commitment to intersectional feminism. She recognized that the struggles for equality and justice were interwoven and could not be separated. Her work emphasized the need to address the complex web of oppressions that marginalized individuals faced, acknowledging that one's identity encompassed multiple facets.

Among her notable works, "The Cancer Journals" stands as a poignant testament to Lorde's ability to merge personal experience with broader social commentary. Her candid exploration of her battle with breast cancer not only shed light on the challenges faced by cancer survivors but also offered a profound meditation on the intersection of illness, identity, and society's expectations.

"Zami: A New Spelling of My Name," Lorde's biomythography, further exemplified her literary prowess. In this seminal work, she chronicled her journey as a Black lesbian woman coming of age in a world that often sought to silence voices like hers. The narrative wove together her personal experiences with a broader exploration of identity, resilience, and the power of storytelling.

Audre Lorde's impact extended beyond the printed page. She was a fierce advocate for social justice, using her platform to elevate the voices of those who had long been silenced. Her commitment to dismantling systems of oppression and discrimination was unwavering.

As we reflect on Audre Lorde's life and work, we are reminded of her enduring influence. Her words continue to inspire activists, writers, and advocates around the world. Her unrelenting dedication to intersectional feminism and social justice serves as a guiding light, urging us all to confront the injustices that persist in our society and to amplify the voices of the marginalized.

Audre Lorde's legacy is not just a tale in the history of literature and activism; it is a call to action. It challenges us to engage in the ongoing struggle for equality, to embrace the complexity of our identities, and to recognize the power of words to effect change. Her work reminds us that in our shared humanity, we find the strength to create a more just and equitable world.

J.K. Rowling: The Magical World of Harry Potter and the Power of Imagination

J.K. Rowling, a name synonymous with literary magic, catapulted herself into the annals of literary history with her creation of the enchanting Harry Potter series. Born in Yate, Gloucestershire, in 1965, Rowling's journey from a struggling writer to a global sensation is a testament to the transformative power of storytelling.

At the heart of Rowling's legacy lies the beloved Harry Potter series, a magical world that has cast its spell on millions of readers across the globe. The saga, centered around the young wizard Harry Potter and his adventures at Hogwarts School of Witchcraft and Wizardry, has become a cultural phenomenon of unparalleled proportions.

What sets Rowling's fantasy novels apart is not just their ability to transport readers to a world of spells, potions, and mythical creatures but also their profound exploration of universal themes. The tales of courage, friendship, and the unyielding fight against discrimination resonate deeply with readers of all ages. Through the characters of Harry, Hermione, Ron, and their companions, Rowling weaves a narrative tapestry that champions the enduring power of human connection and the triumph of good over evil.

The enduring appeal of Rowling's work is evident in its ability to transcend generations. Children and adults alike have been captivated by the magic of Hogwarts, the whimsy of Diagon Alley, and the depth of the wizarding world she meticulously crafted. With each turning page, readers have been transported to a realm where the ordinary becomes extraordinary, where the impossible becomes possible.

Rowling's storytelling prowess has extended beyond the printed page. The Harry Potter books have been adapted into a highly successful film series, further cementing their place in popular culture. The magic has also been felt in theme parks, stage productions, and a myriad of merchandise, all of which allow fans to immerse themselves in the enchanting universe she envisioned.

But perhaps the most enduring impact of J.K. Rowling's work lies in the messages of hope and resilience it imparts. Through the trials and tribulations faced by Harry and his friends, readers are reminded that even in the darkest of times, there is light to be found. The books inspire us to stand up against discrimination and injustice, to believe in the power of friendship, and to summon the courage to confront our own challenges.

As we celebrate the literary legacy of J.K. Rowling, we honor not only her remarkable storytelling but also the profound influence of her work on the imaginations and hearts of readers around the world. Her books continue to serve as a beacon of wonder, a reminder that within the pages of a book, we can discover a world of infinite possibilities and, most importantly, the enduring magic of the human spirit.

Margaret Atwood: Crafting Dystopian Worlds and Provoking Thought

Margaret Atwood, a literary luminary hailing from Ottawa, Canada, has etched her name into the annals of contemporary literature with a distinctive focus on dystopian fiction. Born in 1939, Atwood's imaginative storytelling and thought-provoking narratives have resonated deeply with readers, making her a celebrated author known for her incisive exploration of societal, gender, and political issues.

At the heart of Atwood's literary legacy is "The Handmaid's Tale," a dystopian masterpiece that has left an indelible mark on the literary landscape. This haunting novel unfurls a chilling vision of a future marked by oppression and totalitarianism. Through the lens of her protagonist, Offred, Atwood navigates the treacherous terrain of a society where women's bodies and identities are tightly controlled, where freedom is a distant memory, and where the consequences of rebellion are dire.

While "The Handmaid's Tale" stands as one of her most iconic works, Atwood's exploration of societal and gender issues extends far beyond this singular narrative. Her body of work delves into the complexities of human nature, power dynamics, and the fragility of democracy. She has the rare ability to craft fictional worlds that, while dystopian in nature, shed light on contemporary challenges and prompt introspection.

Atwood's novels serve as incisive mirrors reflecting the anxieties and injustices of our times. They challenge readers to confront uncomfortable truths, to grapple with the consequences of apathy and complacency, and to question the structures that govern our lives. In a world characterized by rapid change and social upheaval, her stories remind us that the line between reality and dystopia can sometimes be unsettlingly thin.

The power of Atwood's writing lies not only in her ability to construct intricate and unsettling worlds but also in her capacity to inspire dialogue and debate. Her novels serve as catalysts for discussions on issues such as gender equality, environmentalism, and the erosion of civil liberties. Through her storytelling, she encourages readers to think critically about the world they inhabit and the future they wish to shape.

As we celebrate Margaret Atwood's literary contributions, we honor not only her talent for crafting dystopian narratives but also her role as a provocateur of thought and discussion. Her works are a testament to the enduring relevance of literature as a medium for exploring the complexities of the human condition and for challenging the status quo. Margaret Atwood reminds us that within the pages of a book, we find not only stories but also the seeds of change and the power to confront the challenges of our time.

Marjane Satrapi: Weaving History and Artistry in "Persepolis"

Marjane Satrapi, the Iranian-born graphic novelist and memoirist, has carved a unique and profound niche in the literary world by intertwining the visual and the autobiographical. Born in Rasht, Iran, in 1969, Satrapi's journey is one of artistic expression and storytelling that resonates deeply with readers around the globe.

At the core of Satrapi's literary oeuvre lies "Persepolis," a graphic novel that serves as a poignant chronicle of her childhood experiences during the tumultuous Iranian Revolution. Through her expressive and evocative artwork, Satrapi offers a vivid window into her formative years, marked by political upheaval, cultural transformation, and personal introspection.

"Persepolis" is a tour de force of graphic literature, where the power of storytelling is magnificently merged with the visual artistry of Satrapi's illustrations. The novel deftly navigates the complexities of growing up in a country undergoing radical change, capturing the innocence, confusion, and resilience of youth against the backdrop of a revolution that would reshape a nation.

One of the defining features of Satrapi's work is her ability to seamlessly blend the personal and the political. Her narrative is not confined to mere historical documentation but transcends into a universal exploration of identity, belonging, and the human spirit's indomitable capacity to endure and adapt.

"Persepolis" is not only a graphic novel but also a testament to the resilience of the human spirit. It is a mirror reflecting the universal struggle for freedom and self-expression, as well as the challenges faced by individuals living under oppressive regimes. Through her storytelling and artistry, Satrapi invites readers to journey with her through the labyrinth of her memories, where the personal becomes a poignant allegory for the collective.

The impact of "Persepolis" extends beyond the pages of the graphic novel. It has been adapted into an animated film, reaching an even broader audience and cementing its status as a significant contribution to both graphic literature and cinematic storytelling. The resonance of Marjane Satrapi's narrative lies in its ability to bridge cultural divides, fostering empathy, and understanding among readers from diverse backgrounds.

In celebrating Marjane Satrapi's work, we honor not only her talent for graphic storytelling but also her role as a bridge-builder between cultures and as a voice for those whose stories often remain untold. Her unique blend of art and autobiography continues to captivate audiences, reminding us of the transformative power of storytelling to illuminate the shared humanity that unites us all. Marjane Satrapi stands as a testament to the enduring legacy of graphic literature as a medium for conveying powerful, universal stories.

Jane Austen: Redefining the Novel

In the quiet parlor rooms of 18th and 19th century England, a literary luminary by the name of Jane Austen crafted stories that would forever reshape the landscape of the novel. With wit, insight, and a keen understanding of human nature, Austen breathed life into her characters and offered astute social commentary, leaving an indelible mark on the world of literature.

Jane Austen was born in Hampshire, England, in 1775, into a family of modest means but with a strong literary tradition. She grew up in a world where novels were emerging as a popular form of entertainment, often dismissed as trivial by the literary elite. However, Austen possessed a remarkable talent for keen observation and a gift for crafting compelling narratives.

Austen's novels are a testament to her sharp intellect and her ability to dissect the society and culture of her time with a satirical pen. Her novels, including "Pride and Prejudice," "Sense and Sensibility," and "Emma," are characterized by astute character studies, social commentary, and a keen sense of humor.

One of Austen's enduring contributions to the novel was her focus on the domestic sphere and the lives of women. Her heroines, like Elizabeth Bennet and Elinor Dashwood, grappled with the limitations placed on women in Regency-era England. These women were not mere damsels in distress but characters with agency, wit, and resilience. Through their experiences, Austen highlighted the challenges and constraints faced by women of her time while subtly advocating for their rights and individuality.

Austen's exploration of themes such as love, marriage, class, and societal expectations resonates across centuries. Her characters navigate the complexities of social hierarchies and personal relationships, providing insights into the human condition that remain relevant to this day. Her novels serve as windows into a bygone era while offering timeless lessons on love, self-discovery, and the importance of character.

One of Austen's remarkable achievements was her narrative style. Her novels were characterized by a free indirect speech, a technique that allowed her to enter the minds of her characters and provide readers with a nuanced understanding of their thoughts and emotions. This narrative innovation allowed readers to intimately connect with her characters and experience the world through their eyes.

Despite her literary prowess, Jane Austen initially published her works anonymously, often under the pseudonym "A Lady." It was not until her brother, Henry Austen, revealed her authorship in the posthumous publication of "Northanger Abbey" and "Persuasion" that her true identity as a novelist emerged.

Jane Austen's novels were not just beloved by her contemporaries; they continue to captivate readers and inspire adaptations, films, and scholarly discussions. Her enduring popularity reflects the timeless quality of her storytelling, her sharp wit, and her ability to delve into the intricacies of human nature.

As we celebrate Jane Austen's contributions to literature, we are reminded of the power of the written word to transcend time and societal norms. Her novels continue to enchant and engage readers worldwide, offering a glimpse into the human experience with all its complexities and contradictions. Jane Austen's legacy endures as a testament to the enduring power of literature to illuminate the human condition.

The impact of Jane Austen's novels extends far beyond the realm of literature; it reverberates through the corridors of culture, challenging conventions and influencing countless writers and thinkers. Her narrative innovations and incisive commentary on society have left an indelible mark on the world of letters and continue to shape the way we perceive the novel.

One of Austen's remarkable achievements was her ability to create indelible characters who felt like real people. Her protagonists, whether it be the spirited Elizabeth Bennet or the sensible Elinor Dashwood, possessed a depth and complexity that set them apart from the one-dimensional heroines of her time. Austen's characters grappled with personal dilemmas, societal pressures, and moral choices, making them relatable to readers across generations.

Austen's novels were not just a reflection of the society in which she lived; they were also a commentary on it. She had an astute eye for the foibles and pretensions of the upper-middle-class society of Regency-era England. Through her wit and satire, she gently but effectively critiqued the conventions, prejudices, and hypocrisies of her time. Her novels exposed the absurdity of valuing wealth and social status over character and integrity.

One of the hallmarks of Austen's writing is her exploration of the theme of marriage. In an era when marriage was often a means of securing financial stability and social standing, Austen's novels stood out for championing the idea of marrying for love and mutual respect. Her heroines sought not just romantic fulfillment but also autonomy and agency in a world that often sought to constrain them.

The enduring appeal of Austen's novels lies in their ability to transcend time and place. While rooted in the societal norms and manners of early 19th-century England, her themes and characters remain universally relatable.

Readers from diverse cultures and backgrounds have found resonance in her stories of love, independence, and the pursuit of happiness.

Austen's literary legacy has continued to thrive in the centuries since her novels were first published. Her influence can be seen in the works of subsequent generations of writers, from the Brontë sisters to contemporary novelists like Zadie Smith and Helen Fielding. Adaptations of her novels into film and television have introduced her stories to new audiences, ensuring that her characters and themes remain fresh and relevant.

Moreover, Austen's works have inspired a thriving community of scholars, creating a rich tapestry of academic research and critical analysis. Her novels have been scrutinized for their narrative techniques, feminist themes, and cultural significance, adding depth to our understanding of her contributions to literature.

As we reflect on the legacy of Jane Austen, we are reminded of the enduring power of literature to challenge norms, provoke thought, and provide solace to readers. Her novels continue to offer insight into the human experience, transcending time and place to connect with readers on a profound level.

In celebrating Jane Austen's work, we honor not only her literary genius but also her courage to write with a clear voice in an era when female authors often faced societal constraints. Her legacy serves as an inspiration to writers and readers alike, encouraging us to explore the complexities of human nature and society through the pages of a well-crafted novel.

Maya Angelou: Inspiring with her Poetry and Memoirs

The name Maya Angelou shines as a beacon of resilience, creativity, and profound human insight. Through her poetry, memoirs, and eloquent storytelling, she not only captured the essence of the African American experience but also touched the hearts of readers worldwide, inspiring them to rise above adversity and celebrate the indomitable spirit of the human soul.

Maya Angelou was born Marguerite Annie Johnson on April 4, 1928, in St. Louis, Missouri. Her early years were marked by upheaval and hardship. Raised by her grandmother in the racially segregated South, Angelou faced the harsh realities of racism and discrimination from a young age. Her experiences during these formative years would later inform her writing and advocacy for civil rights.

At the heart of Angelou's literary legacy lies her profound ability to give voice to the human condition. Her debut memoir, "I Know Why the Caged Bird Sings," published in 1969, stands as a powerful testament to her resilience in the face of adversity. The book, which recounts her early life and coming-of-age, remains a landmark work in African American literature and a classic in the genre of autobiography.

"I Know Why the Caged Bird Sings" is a poignant exploration of Angelou's journey from a traumatized young girl to a self-possessed young woman. Through lyrical prose, she grapples with themes of identity, race, sexual abuse, and the quest for self-acceptance. The title itself, borrowed from a poem by Paul Laurence Dunbar, encapsulates the yearning for freedom and self-expression that pervades the narrative.

Angelou's ability to convey the emotional depth of her experiences resonated deeply with readers, who found solace and inspiration in her words. Her willingness to confront the painful aspects of her past and share her vulnerabilities was an act of courage and empathy that transcended the confines of literature.

In addition to her memoirs, Maya Angelou's poetry evoked the rhythms of life, love, and the human spirit. Her collection "And Still I Rise," published in 1978, remains a testament to her mastery of verse and her ability to uplift the human soul. Through poems like "Phenomenal Woman" and "Still I Rise," she celebrated the strength and resilience of women and marginalized communities, instilling in them a sense of pride and self-worth.

Angelou's impact extended beyond the written word. Her dynamic presence as a speaker, performer, and civil rights activist brought her message of hope and empowerment to audiences around the world. She used her platform to advocate for social justice and civil rights, working alongside figures like Martin Luther King Jr. and Malcolm X.

Throughout her life, Maya Angelou received numerous awards and honors, including the Presidential Medal of Freedom and the National Medal of Arts. Her contributions to literature and her commitment to social justice continue to inspire generations of writers, activists, and readers.

As we celebrate Maya Angelou's legacy, we are reminded of the transformative power of storytelling and the ability of words to heal, inspire, and connect us across the boundaries of time, race, and circumstance. Her life and work stand as a testament to the enduring spirit of resilience, courage, and the belief in the potential for positive change.

In honoring Maya Angelou, we honor not only her literary genius but also her unwavering dedication to amplifying the voices of the marginalized and her ceaseless efforts to make the world a more inclusive and compassionate place.

Virginia Woolf: Challenging Literary Conventions

In the early 20th century, amidst a literary landscape dominated by traditional narrative forms, Virginia Woolf emerged as a revolutionary force, reshaping the boundaries of fiction and challenging established conventions. Through her groundbreaking works, she pioneered the stream of consciousness narrative style and explored the inner lives of her characters with unparalleled depth and innovation.

Born Adeline Virginia Stephen on January 25, 1882, in London, Virginia Woolf was raised in an intellectual and artistic environment. Her upbringing exposed her to the ideas of feminism, modernism, and the literary avant-garde, which would later influence her own writing.

Woolf's novels, including "Mrs. Dalloway," "To the Lighthouse," and "Orlando," are celebrated for their narrative experimentation and their exploration of the inner workings of the human mind. Her use of the stream of consciousness technique allowed readers to delve into the thoughts, memories, and perceptions of her characters in a way that had not been done before.

One of Woolf's most renowned works, "Mrs. Dalloway," published in 1925, is a prime example of her narrative innovation. The novel takes place over the course of a single day and follows the inner monologues of its characters, particularly the titular character, Clarissa Dalloway. Through Woolf's lyrical prose and fluid transitions between characters' perspectives, she presents a layered and nuanced portrayal of consciousness itself.

"To the Lighthouse," published in 1927, is another masterpiece of Woolf's stream of consciousness style. In this novel, she delves into the minds of the Ramsay family as they vacation at their family home on the Isle of Skye. Through her exploration of their inner thoughts and emotions, Woolf captures the fleeting nature of time and the complexities of human relationships.

Woolf's bold narrative choices were not merely stylistic experiments; they were a reflection of her deep interest in the inner lives of her characters and her desire to convey the subjective nature of human experience. Her works rejected the conventions of linear storytelling and invited readers to grapple with the complexities of memory, perception, and the passage of time.

In addition to her narrative innovation, Virginia Woolf was a key figure in the Bloomsbury Group, a collective of intellectuals, writers, and artists who engaged in discussions about literature, art, and society. This intellectual milieu influenced her work and allowed her to engage with progressive ideas, including feminism and pacifism.

Woolf's feminist perspective is evident in her essay "A Room of One's Own," published in 1929. In it, she argues for the importance of women having financial independence and a physical space in which to create, asserting that these conditions are essential for women to produce great literature. Her essay remains a cornerstone of feminist literary criticism.

Tragically, Woolf battled mental health issues throughout her life, and she ultimately took her own life in 1941. Her struggles with mental illness cast a somber light on the societal pressures and limitations faced by women of her time.

Virginia Woolf's impact on literature and the modernist movement cannot be overstated. Her experimental narrative techniques and exploration of the inner psyche continue to inspire writers and readers alike. Her legacy challenges us to question established conventions, to embrace innovation, and to delve deep into the complexities of human existence.

As we commemorate Virginia Woolf's contributions to literature, we celebrate her role as a trailblazer who expanded the possibilities of storytelling and gave voice to the rich tapestry of human consciousness.

Toni Morrison: Exploring African American Experiences

In the realm of American literature, Toni Morrison stands as a towering figure, whose unparalleled storytelling and lyrical prose have illuminated the African American experience with unparalleled depth, empathy, and complexity. Through her novels, she explored the legacies of slavery, the complexities of identity, and the enduring power of love and community.

Toni Morrison, born Chloe Ardelia Wofford on February 18, 1931, in Lorain, Ohio, possessed a unique ability to weave together history, folklore, and personal narratives into a tapestry of storytelling that transcended genres and captivated readers around the world. Her novels are not just literary works; they are profound meditations on the human condition.

One of Morrison's most celebrated novels, "Beloved," published in 1987, is a masterpiece that delves into the enduring trauma of slavery. Set in the post-Civil War era, the novel tells the story of Sethe, a former slave who escapes to freedom but is haunted by the ghost of her infant daughter, whom she killed to spare her from a life of slavery. "Beloved" explores the psychological scars left by slavery and the desperate lengths to which individuals will go to protect their loved ones.

Morrison's narrative prowess shines through in "Song of Solomon," published in 1977. This novel follows the journey of Macon "Milkman" Dead III as he embarks on a quest to discover his family's history and his own identity. Through rich storytelling and vivid characters, Morrison explores themes of flight, family, and the search for selfhood. The novel is a lyrical exploration of African American folklore and the complexities of generational legacies.

In "The Bluest Eye," Morrison's debut novel published in 1970, she examines the destructive effects of racial self-loathing and societal beauty standards on a young African American girl named Pecola Breedlove. Through this poignant and unsettling narrative, Morrison lays bare the harsh realities of racism and the deep-seated wounds it inflicts on individuals and communities.

Morrison's storytelling often defied linear chronology, instead opting for nonlinear narratives that mirrored the complexities of memory and history. Her prose was rich with symbolism and allegory, inviting readers to engage with her narratives on multiple levels. Her work was characterized by its unflinching honesty and its ability to challenge readers to confront uncomfortable truths about race, identity, and power.

In 1993, Toni Morrison became the first African American woman to be awarded the Nobel Prize in Literature. The Nobel Committee cited her novels as "characterized by visionary force and poetic import, giving life to an essential aspect of American reality." Her contributions to literature went beyond storytelling; they were acts of reclamation and celebration of African American history and culture.

Morrison's novels continue to be widely read and studied in classrooms and book clubs, sparking discussions about race, identity, and the enduring legacy of slavery in America. Her influence on contemporary literature is immeasurable, as she inspired a new generation of writers to explore the complexities of the African American experience.

Toni Morrison's legacy challenges us to confront the painful aspects of our history and to acknowledge the enduring struggles of marginalized communities. Her novels remind us of the transformative power of literature to shed light on the human experience and to inspire empathy and understanding.

As we celebrate Toni Morrison's contributions to literature, we honor her role as a storyteller, a chronicler of African American history, and a literary luminary whose work continues to resonate with readers, transcending time and place.

Chapter 3: Female Leaders of Nations

Sonia Gandhi: A Resilient Leader Shaping India's Political Landscape

Sonia Gandhi, a prominent figure in Indian politics, has etched her name into the annals of leadership through her unwavering commitment to the Indian National Congress and her influential role in shaping the nation's political discourse. Born in Italy in 1946 and later becoming an Indian citizen, Gandhi's journey from a private life to a central figure in Indian politics is a story of resilience and dedication.

Sonia Gandhi's tenure as the President of the Indian National Congress marked a pivotal era in the party's history. Her leadership brought stability and direction to a party with a rich legacy, guiding it through challenging political landscapes and electoral battles. Under her stewardship, the party played a vital role in the nation's governance, advocating for policies that reflected its vision for India's development and growth.

Gandhi's influence extended beyond her party's leadership; it resonated throughout the nation's political landscape. Her presence in Indian politics brought forth spirited debates and discussions, influencing national policies and shaping the political narrative. Her measured and principled approach to governance earned her respect from both allies and opponents.

Sonia Gandhi's dedication to social and political causes remains a defining aspect of her leadership. Her advocacy for social justice, women's empowerment, and the rights of marginalized communities has been unwavering. She has championed policies that address poverty alleviation, healthcare, and education, reflecting her commitment to improving the lives of ordinary citizens.

Throughout her political journey, Sonia Gandhi has faced both accolades and challenges. She has navigated the complex terrain of Indian politics with grace and determination, earning a place of significance in the nation's political history. Her leadership style, characterized by pragmatism and a deep sense of duty, has left an indelible mark on the country's political landscape.

As we reflect on Sonia Gandhi's contributions to Indian politics, we honor not only her leadership but also her dedication to social and political causes. Her legacy serves as a reminder of the transformative potential of leadership, where individuals, driven by their principles and commitment, can shape the destiny of nations and advocate for the betterment of society. Sonia Gandhi stands as an exemplar of leadership that is rooted in service and the pursuit of a brighter, more inclusive future for all.

Cleopatra: Shaping Ancient Egypt's Destiny

In the annals of history, few figures have captured the imagination and fascination of the world like Cleopatra, the last Pharaoh of ancient Egypt. Her reign, marked by intrigue, romance, and political maneuvering, played a pivotal role in the fate of Egypt and its interactions with the Roman Republic.

Cleopatra VII Philopator, born in 69 BCE, ascended to the throne of Egypt at a time of immense political turmoil. Egypt, a powerful and culturally rich kingdom, was caught in the crosscurrents of Roman expansion in the eastern Mediterranean. Cleopatra's reign was characterized by her shrewd diplomacy, intelligence, and ambition to protect and preserve her kingdom's sovereignty.

One of Cleopatra's most enduring legacies is her relationship with prominent Roman leaders, including Julius Caesar and Mark Antony. In 48 BCE, she formed a romantic and political alliance with Julius Caesar, who was at the height of his power. Their relationship resulted in the birth of a son, Caesarion, and established Cleopatra as a key player in Roman politics.

After Julius Caesar's assassination in 44 BCE, Cleopatra aligned herself with Mark Antony, a member of the Second Triumvirate, which ruled Rome. Her relationship with Antony, both romantic and political, marked a significant chapter in her life. Together, they formed an alliance against Octavian, another member of the Triumvirate, in the struggle for control of Rome.

However, the Battle of Actium in 31 BCE marked the downfall of Cleopatra and Antony. Octavian emerged victorious, and fearing capture, Cleopatra and Antony took their own lives. This event marked the end of the Ptolemaic dynasty and the annexation of Egypt by Rome, as Octavian became the first Roman Emperor, Augustus.

Cleopatra's life and legacy have been the subject of countless works of art, literature, and film, each interpreting her story in their own way. Her image has been romanticized and vilified, making her one of history's most enigmatic and controversial figures.

Beyond her romantic associations, Cleopatra was a capable and strategic ruler. She sought to strengthen Egypt's economy, administration, and military defenses. Her reign also witnessed cultural and artistic flourishing, with the blending of Greek and Egyptian influences, known as the Hellenistic period.

Cleopatra's story resonates with themes of power, ambition, and the complexities of leadership. Her role as a female ruler in a male-dominated world challenged societal norms and expectations. She navigated treacherous political waters with intelligence and determination, striving to protect the interests of her kingdom.

As we reflect on Cleopatra's life and reign, we are reminded of the enduring fascination with her story and the influence she exerted on the course of history. Her legacy continues to inspire discussions about leadership, diplomacy, and the complexities of identity and power.

In celebrating Cleopatra's contributions to ancient Egypt and her enduring impact on global culture, we honor her role as a symbol of resilience, leadership, and the enduring allure of historical enigma.

Queen Elizabeth I: Establishing the Elizabethan Era

In the annals of history, few monarchs have left as indelible a mark as Queen Elizabeth I of England. Her reign, known as the Elizabethan era, is celebrated for its cultural flourishing, maritime exploration, and the establishment of England as a formidable global power. Elizabeth I's leadership and vision transformed a nation and shaped the course of history.

Elizabeth Tudor was born on September 7, 1533, to King Henry VIII of England and his second wife, Anne Boleyn. Her early life was marked by political turmoil, as her mother's marriage to Henry led to the English Reformation and the establishment of the Church of England. Elizabeth's claim to the throne was tenuous, given the tumultuous nature of her father's reign and the shifting religious and political landscape of Europe.

Upon her ascent to the throne in 1558, Elizabeth I faced a kingdom deeply divided by religious conflicts, economic challenges, and external threats. Her reign was characterized by a series of profound decisions and policies that would come to define the Elizabethan era.

One of Elizabeth's most significant achievements was her establishment of religious stability in England. Her religious settlement, enshrined in the Act of Uniformity and the Elizabethan Religious Settlement, allowed for a moderate and pragmatic approach to religion. It sought to strike a balance between Catholic and Protestant factions, emphasizing the importance of state loyalty over religious allegiance. This policy brought a degree of religious peace to England and set the stage for the development of Anglicanism.

Elizabeth's reign also witnessed a period of remarkable cultural flourishing. The Elizabethan era is renowned for its contributions to literature, theater, and the arts. It was during this time that William Shakespeare, Christopher Marlowe, and other playwrights and poets produced their masterpieces, creating a literary legacy that endures to this day. The construction of the Globe Theatre in London marked a golden age of English theater.

Elizabeth's support for exploration and overseas expansion laid the foundation for England's emergence as a global power. The voyages of explorers like Sir Walter Raleigh, Sir Francis Drake, and Sir John Hawkins expanded English influence and trade routes, ushering in the age of exploration.

One of the most iconic events of Elizabeth's reign was the defeat of the Spanish Armada in 1588. The Spanish Armada's failed invasion of England bolstered English national pride and cemented Elizabeth's reputation as a strong and capable leader. Her famous speech at Tilbury, where she rallied her troops in the face of imminent invasion, remains a symbol of her leadership and determination.

Despite her numerous accomplishments, Elizabeth's reign was not without challenges. Her refusal to marry and produce an heir led to concerns about the succession of the English throne. Additionally, her rule was marked by political intrigue, including the execution of her cousin Mary, Queen of Scots, who posed a threat to Elizabeth's throne.

Queen Elizabeth I's death in 1603 marked the end of an era, as she left behind a legacy of cultural achievement, political stability, and international influence. Her reign is remembered as a time of remarkable transformation and achievement, and she remains one of England's most iconic and beloved monarchs.

As we celebrate Queen Elizabeth I's contributions to England and her enduring impact on global history, we honor her role as a visionary leader who navigated the complexities of her era with wisdom, pragmatism, and a profound commitment to her nation's welfare.

Indira Gandhi: Pioneering Female Leadership in India

In the history of modern India, the name Indira Gandhi stands as a symbol of resilience, leadership, and pioneering female empowerment. As India's first and, to date, only female Prime Minister, she navigated the complexities of a diverse and dynamic nation, leaving an indelible mark on its political landscape and societal norms.

Indira Priyadarshini Nehru was born on November 19, 1917, into a family deeply involved in India's struggle for independence from British colonial rule. Her father, Jawaharlal Nehru, was a prominent leader in the Indian National Congress and would later become India's first Prime Minister. Her upbringing in a politically charged environment shaped her worldview and ignited her passion for public service.

Indira Gandhi's early years were marked by her involvement in the Indian independence movement. She witnessed firsthand the sacrifices made by her family and countless others in the pursuit of freedom and self-determination. Her experiences during this period instilled in her a sense of duty and a commitment to the welfare of the Indian people.

Her political journey accelerated when she became a member of the Indian National Congress, the party at the forefront of India's struggle for independence. Her leadership qualities and dedication were quickly recognized, leading to her appointment as the President of the Indian National Congress in 1959.

In 1966, following the death of Prime Minister Lal Bahadur Shastri, Indira Gandhi assumed the office of Prime Minister, becoming India's first female head of government. Her tenure was marked by a series of significant challenges, both domestic and international.

One of her most notable achievements was the successful conduct of the Bangladesh Liberation War in 1971, which led to the creation of the independent nation of Bangladesh. India's support for the Bangladeshi independence movement and its military intervention in the conflict underscored India's commitment to regional stability and its advocacy for the principles of self-determination.

However, her leadership also faced internal challenges, including economic difficulties, political opposition, and social unrest. The period of her rule from 1975 to 1977, known as the Emergency, saw the suspension of civil liberties and the curtailment of political freedoms. While she argued that it was necessary to maintain order and implement necessary reforms, her decision to declare the Emergency was met with criticism and protests.

In 1977, Indira Gandhi's government was voted out of power, marking a brief hiatus in her political career. Nevertheless, she returned to office in 1980, winning a landslide victory in the general elections.

Her second term as Prime Minister witnessed both achievements and challenges. She grappled with complex issues such as insurgency in the Punjab region and the assassination of her son Sanjay Gandhi. Her leadership style remained assertive and unapologetic, and she continued to pursue policies aimed at social justice, economic development, and India's strategic interests.

Tragically, Indira Gandhi's life came to a tragic end on October 31, 1984, when she was assassinated by her own bodyguards in retaliation for the Operation Blue Star military operation in the Golden Temple in Amritsar, Punjab.

Indira Gandhi's legacy is complex and multifaceted. She was a trailblazer who shattered the gender barrier in Indian politics and inspired generations of women to enter public service. Her leadership left a lasting impact on India's political landscape, and her commitment to social justice and economic development continues to influence policy discussions in India.

As we commemorate Indira Gandhi's contributions to India and her pioneering role as a female leader in a male-dominated field, we honor her legacy as a symbol of strength, determination, and the enduring possibilities of female leadership.

Angela Merkel: Shaping Modern European Politics

In the 21st century, Angela Merkel emerged as a towering figure in global politics, shaping the trajectory of not only her native Germany but also the European Union and the world at large. As the first woman to serve as Chancellor of Germany and one of the longest-serving leaders in modern European history, Merkel's leadership exemplified pragmatism, steady diplomacy, and a commitment to European unity.

Angela Dorothea Kasner was born on July 17, 1954, in Hamburg, West Germany. Raised in East Germany, she experienced the realities of a divided nation and witnessed the fall of the Berlin Wall in 1989, which ultimately led to German reunification. Her early career as a physicist and research scientist provided her with a strong analytical background, a quality that would become a hallmark of her political leadership.

Merkel's political journey began in the wake of the reunification of Germany, as she joined the Christian Democratic Union (CDU) and quickly rose through the ranks. In 2005, she made history when she became Germany's first female Chancellor, a position she would hold for four consecutive terms, making her one of the most influential political leaders of the 21st century.

Merkel's leadership was characterized by pragmatism and stability. Her approach to governance emphasized fiscal responsibility, economic stability, and a commitment to European integration. During her tenure, Germany became known as the economic powerhouse of Europe, weathering global financial crises with resilience.

One of the defining moments of Merkel's leadership was her response to the European financial crisis of 2008. She played a central role in negotiating bailout packages for struggling Eurozone countries and advocated for fiscal discipline and structural reforms. Her leadership during this turbulent period was instrumental in stabilizing the European economy.

Merkel's handling of the European migrant crisis in 2015 was another significant chapter in her political career. Faced with a wave of refugees fleeing conflict and hardship, she advocated for a compassionate and coordinated response within the European Union. While her decision to open Germany's borders to refugees garnered both praise and criticism, it underscored her commitment to humanitarian values and European solidarity.

Throughout her tenure, Merkel was known for her steady and pragmatic approach to international diplomacy. She played a key role in negotiations with Russia, particularly regarding the Ukraine crisis and energy policy. Her leadership in the European Union bolstered the bloc's stability and cohesion, even as it faced challenges such as Brexit.

Merkel's leadership style was often described as cautious and analytical, earning her the nickname "Mutti," or "Mom," among Germans. Her ability to navigate complex political terrain, build consensus, and maintain a measured approach to crises contributed to her popularity and respect both at home and abroad.

In 2021, Angela Merkel stepped down as Chancellor, leaving a legacy of stability, economic strength, and European cooperation. Her leadership demonstrated the enduring importance of pragmatism and diplomacy in a rapidly changing world.

As we commemorate Angela Merkel's contributions to Germany, Europe, and global politics, we honor her role as a trailblazer who defied gender stereotypes, a steadfast leader who guided her nation through challenging times, and a symbol of the enduring possibilities of leadership grounded in reason and responsibility.

Chapter 4: Trailblazing Women in Civil Rights

Eva Perón: A Champion of Social Justice and Equality

Eva Perón, affectionately known as "Evita," stands as an enduring symbol of compassion, advocacy, and social justice in Argentine history. Born in 1919 in Los Toldos, Argentina, her journey from a humble background to becoming a revered First Lady is a testament to her unwavering dedication to improving the lives of women and the working class.

At the heart of Eva Perón's legacy lies her fervent advocacy for labor rights and women's suffrage. As the First Lady of Argentina, she leveraged her position to champion causes that had long been overlooked and marginalized. Her leadership brought about transformative changes that improved the lives of countless Argentines.

One of Eva Perón's most significant achievements was her instrumental role in securing women's right to vote in Argentina in 1947. Her tireless efforts in advocating for women's suffrage marked a watershed moment in the country's history and underscored her commitment to gender equality and representation.

Beyond her work for women's rights, Eva Perón was a tireless advocate for the working class. She established the Eva Perón Foundation, which focused on providing social welfare programs, healthcare, and education to the most vulnerable segments of society. Her commitment to uplifting the poor and marginalized earned her the love and admiration of countless Argentines.

Eva Perón's legacy endures not only for her advocacy but also for the profound impact she had on the lives of the people she served. Her efforts were deeply rooted in compassion, and she often personally intervened to help those in need. Her connection with the people was palpable, and she became a beloved figure in Argentine history.

In recognition of her tireless work and dedication, Eva Perón is often referred to as "Evita" by the Argentine people. Her legacy continues to serve as a powerful symbol of social justice, compassion, and the capacity for positive change.

As we celebrate Eva Perón's life and contributions, we honor not only her advocacy but also her indomitable spirit and her lasting impact on the pursuit of equality and social justice. She reminds us that individuals, through their dedication and empathy, can make a profound difference in the lives of others and leave an enduring legacy that transcends time. Eva Perón remains an inspiration to those who champion the cause of social justice and equality.

Gloria Steinem: Pioneering Feminism and Shaping Social Change

Gloria Steinem, an iconic figure in the realm of feminism and social-political activism, has left an indelible mark on the quest for gender equality, reproductive rights, and women's liberation. Born in Toledo, Ohio, in 1934, Steinem's journey through advocacy and journalism has played a pivotal role in reshaping the landscape of women's rights.

At the heart of Gloria Steinem's legacy lies her unyielding dedication to the cause of feminism. As a prominent feminist and social-political activist, she dedicated her life to challenging gender norms and advocating for the rights of women. Her advocacy encompassed a wide range of issues, from reproductive rights to workplace equality, illuminating the multifaceted nature of the feminist struggle.

One of Steinem's most enduring contributions to the feminist movement was her co-founding of Ms. magazine in 1972. This groundbreaking publication provided a platform for feminist voices and perspectives, sparking essential conversations about gender, discrimination, and societal expectations. Ms. magazine quickly became an influential force in shaping feminist literature and discourse.

Gloria Steinem's impact on the feminist movement extended beyond the pages of Ms. magazine. Her speeches, writings, and activism galvanized a generation of women to demand equality, justice, and agency over their own bodies. She played a central role in advocating for reproductive rights, including access to birth control and safe, legal abortion, and fought against the societal stigma surrounding these issues.

Steinem's activism helped shape the feminist movement in the United States, bringing the struggles and aspirations of women to the forefront of national consciousness. She challenged prevailing stereotypes, disrupted societal norms, and offered a vision of a world where gender equality was not only a goal but a fundamental right.

As we celebrate the life and work of Gloria Steinem, we honor not only her pioneering spirit but also her enduring commitment to the betterment of society. Her activism reminds us of the transformative power of grassroots movements, the importance of elevating marginalized voices, and the capacity for social change through collective action. Gloria Steinem's legacy is a testament to the ongoing struggle for gender equality and the indomitable spirit of those who work tirelessly to reshape the world for the better.

Rigoberta Menchú: Championing Indigenous Rights and Global Inspiration

Rigoberta Menchú, a tireless advocate for indigenous rights and social justice, hails from the heart of Guatemala. Born in 1959 into the Quiché Maya indigenous community, Menchú's life journey is a testament to her unwavering dedication to the rights and well-being of indigenous peoples worldwide.

At the core of Menchú's remarkable legacy is her tireless work as an indigenous rights activist. Her advocacy, rooted in her own experiences as a young Maya woman facing discrimination and marginalization, resonated with indigenous communities not only in Guatemala but also across the globe.

In 1992, Rigoberta Menchú was awarded the Nobel Peace Prize for her relentless efforts in advancing indigenous rights and social justice. Her recognition on the international stage brought attention to the systemic injustices faced by indigenous communities, particularly in Guatemala, and amplified their calls for equality, land rights, and cultural preservation.

Menchú's work extended far beyond the Nobel Prize, as she continued to be a powerful voice for indigenous peoples in the face of adversity. She has been instrumental in raising awareness about the impact of armed conflicts and social inequalities on indigenous communities, shedding light on the struggles they endure.

One of the most significant aspects of Menchú's advocacy is her ability to bridge divides and foster dialogue between indigenous and non-indigenous communities. She has championed the importance of cultural diversity and the preservation of indigenous languages and traditions, emphasizing the rich tapestry of humanity's heritage.

Rigoberta Menchú's influence reverberates globally, serving as an inspiration to indigenous movements and social justice activists. Her commitment to amplifying indigenous voices, advocating for their rights, and challenging the status quo has ignited a beacon of hope for marginalized communities worldwide.

As we celebrate Rigoberta Menchú's life and work, we honor not only her unwavering dedication to indigenous rights but also her enduring legacy as a global inspiration. Her tireless efforts remind us of the importance of recognizing and respecting the rights and dignity of indigenous peoples, and her story serves as a powerful reminder that one individual's passion and perseverance can make a profound impact on the world. Rigoberta Menchú stands as a symbol of resilience, unity, and the ongoing struggle for social justice and indigenous rights.

Rosa Parks: Igniting the Montgomery Bus Boycott

In the annals of the civil rights movement, the name Rosa Parks shines as a symbol of courage, resistance, and the power of a single act of defiance to spark a movement. Her refusal to give up her seat on a segregated bus in Montgomery, Alabama, in 1955 ignited the Montgomery Bus Boycott, a pivotal moment in the struggle for racial equality in the United States.

Rosa Louise McCauley Parks was born on February 4, 1913, in Tuskegee, Alabama. Her early life was marked by the racial segregation and discrimination that defined the Jim Crow South. Parks grew up with a strong sense of justice and a determination to challenge the unjust laws that enforced racial segregation.

On December 1, 1955, Rosa Parks boarded a city bus in Montgomery after a long day of work. When the bus became crowded, the driver instructed Parks and other African American passengers to give up their seats to white passengers, a common practice under the city's segregation laws. Parks, tired of giving in to the degrading and discriminatory system, refused to comply.

Her refusal to move to the back of the bus led to her arrest, sparking outrage and frustration within Montgomery's African American community. That evening, a group of local leaders, including Dr. Martin Luther King Jr., organized a meeting to discuss a plan of action. This meeting marked the beginning of the Montgomery Bus Boycott, a coordinated effort to protest segregation on the city's buses.

For 381 days, African Americans in Montgomery boycotted the city's buses, choosing to walk, carpool, or use alternative means of transportation. The boycott was a testament to the resilience and determination of the African American community in the face of systemic racism. Rosa Parks, with her quiet act of defiance, had become a symbol of the struggle for civil rights.

The Montgomery Bus Boycott not only placed economic pressure on the bus company but also drew national and international attention to the injustice of segregation. The Supreme Court's ruling in the case of Browder v. Gayle in 1956 declared Alabama's bus segregation laws unconstitutional, marking a significant victory for the civil rights movement.

Rosa Parks's actions transcended the Montgomery Bus Boycott, as she became a prominent figure in the civil rights movement. She continued her activism, advocating for desegregation, voter registration, and social justice. Her work extended beyond Montgomery, influencing the broader struggle for civil rights and inspiring others to take a stand against injustice.

Parks's legacy goes beyond her role in the Montgomery Bus Boycott. She symbolizes the power of ordinary individuals to effect change through acts of conscience and courage. Her unwavering commitment to justice and equality serves as a beacon of hope and inspiration for generations to come.

In 1999, Rosa Parks was awarded the Congressional Gold Medal, the highest civilian honor in the United States, in recognition of her pivotal role in the civil rights movement. She passed away on October 24, 2005, leaving behind a legacy of courage, dignity, and the enduring belief that a single act of defiance can ignite a movement and change the course of history.

As we commemorate Rosa Parks's contributions to the civil rights movement and her enduring impact on the struggle for equality, we honor her role as a trailblazer who refused to yield to injustice and who, through her actions, helped to bend the arc of history toward justice.

Harriet Tubman: Guiding Slaves to Freedom on the Underground Railroad

In the annals of American history, Harriet Tubman shines as a beacon of courage, determination, and the unwavering commitment to the cause of freedom. Born into slavery, she escaped to freedom and then risked her life countless times to guide others to liberty through the Underground Railroad, leaving an indelible mark on the struggle for abolition and civil rights.

Harriet Tubman, born Araminta Ross in Dorchester County, Maryland, in the early 1820s, experienced the horrors of slavery from a young age. The brutality and dehumanization of slavery left an enduring impact on her, and she longed for freedom and justice.

In 1849, Tubman made the daring decision to escape slavery, embarking on a journey that would lead her to freedom in the North. Her journey was fraught with peril, as she navigated treacherous terrain and eluded slave catchers. Tubman's escape was not only an act of personal liberation but the beginning of a lifetime dedicated to helping others gain their freedom.

Tubman's remarkable work as a "conductor" on the Underground Railroad earned her legendary status. The Underground Railroad was a network of safe houses and secret routes used to help enslaved individuals escape to freedom in the North or Canada. Tubman became one of its most fearless and effective conductors.

Over the course of approximately a decade, Tubman made numerous journeys back into the South, risking her life to guide enslaved people to freedom. Her missions involved traveling by night, using the North Star as a guide, and relying on her deep knowledge of the land to avoid detection. She became known as "Moses" among those she helped, as she led them from the darkness of slavery to the light of freedom.

Tubman's tireless efforts resulted in the liberation of hundreds of enslaved individuals, including family members and friends. Her work demonstrated not only her bravery but also her unwavering commitment to the cause of abolition and the belief that all people deserved to live free.

During the Civil War, Tubman continued her service, working as a nurse, cook, and spy for the Union Army. She also served as a scout, using her knowledge of the South to gather valuable intelligence. Her contributions to the Union cause and her advocacy for African American soldiers earned her recognition and respect.

After the Civil War, Tubman continued to champion civil rights and women's suffrage. She worked alongside figures such as Susan B. Anthony and Elizabeth Cady Stanton in the fight for women's right to vote.

Harriet Tubman's legacy is one of courage, sacrifice, and determination. Her life and work serve as a testament to the resilience of the human spirit and the power of one individual to effect profound change. Tubman's legacy continues to inspire generations of activists and advocates for civil rights and social justice.

In 2020, it was announced that Harriet Tubman's image would grace the front of the U.S. twenty-dollar bill, making her the first African American and the first woman to appear on U.S. paper currency.

As we commemorate Harriet Tubman's contributions to the abolitionist movement and the cause of freedom, we honor her role as a trailblazer who led others out of darkness and into the promise of a better future.

Chapter 5: Remarkable Women in the Arts

Marina Abramović: Pushing Boundaries in Art and the Human Experience

Marina Abramović, a trailblazing performance artist, has redefined the boundaries of art and the human body through her groundbreaking and often provocative works. Born in Belgrade, Yugoslavia, in 1946, Abramović's artistic journey has consistently challenged conventional notions of art, pushing the limits of physical and psychological endurance.

At the heart of Marina Abramović's legacy is her unwavering commitment to using her body as a canvas and a vessel for artistic exploration. Her performances have taken her to the edges of human experience, subjecting herself to physical pain, exhaustion, and intense emotional vulnerability in the pursuit of art. Through her daring and often controversial works, she has invited audiences to confront the boundaries of their own comfort zones and engage with the raw essence of the human condition.

Abramović's art delves into profound themes of endurance, identity, and spirituality. Her performances are immersive experiences that invite viewers to witness, and sometimes participate in, her transformative artistic rituals. Whether she is sitting in silence for hours, locking eyes with strangers in "The Artist Is Present," or reenacting arduous tasks from her past in "The Artist Is Present," her work serves as a reflection on the nature of existence and the depths of human consciousness.

One of Marina Abramović's most iconic and challenging works was "The Artist Is Present," where she sat motionless for 736 hours at the Museum of Modern Art in New York City, inviting visitors to sit across from her and share a silent moment of connection. This profound act of presence and vulnerability captivated audiences and prompted deep contemplation about the power of human connection and the significance of the present moment.

Throughout her career, Abramović has left an indelible mark on the world of contemporary art. Her daring and thought-provoking performances have inspired a new generation of artists to push the boundaries of their own creative expression. She has received numerous awards and honors for her contributions to the arts and remains a luminary figure in the realm of performance art.

As we celebrate Marina Abramović's artistic journey, we honor not only her boundary-pushing artistry but also her profound influence on the way we perceive and engage with art and the human experience. Her legacy challenges us to question, to explore, and to embrace the transformative potential of art in all its forms. Marina Abramović continues to be an enigmatic and trailblazing figure in the world of contemporary art, reminding us of the boundless possibilities that exist at the intersection of creativity and the human spirit.

Ella Fitzgerald: The First Lady of Song and a Jazz Legend

Ella Fitzgerald, celebrated as one of the greatest jazz vocalists of all time, graced the world with her remarkable voice and talent, earning her the well-deserved title of the "First Lady of Song." Born in Newport News, Virginia, in 1917, Fitzgerald's journey through the world of music is a testament to her unparalleled artistry and enduring influence.

At the heart of Ella Fitzgerald's legacy lies her extraordinary voice, which has been described as a marvel of tone, control, and emotional depth. With a vocal range that spanned three octaves, she had the rare ability to captivate audiences with her velvet-smooth phrasing, impeccable timing, and effortless improvisation. Her voice transcended genres, effortlessly navigating jazz, swing, blues, and ballads, leaving an indelible mark on each.

Fitzgerald's music is a testament to her versatility as an artist. Her interpretations of jazz standards and her collaborations with legendary musicians like Duke Ellington, Count Basie, and Louis Armstrong showcased her ability to elevate any song to a higher plane of artistry. Her scat singing, in particular, became legendary, setting a standard that few could match.

Ella Fitzgerald's influence on the world of music extends far beyond her own recordings. Her impeccable technique, musicality, and emotive delivery have inspired generations of musicians, vocalists, and performers. Her renditions of classic songs like "Summertime," "Mack the Knife," and "I Can't Give You Anything But Love" continue to be cherished by listeners of all ages.

Throughout her career, Ella Fitzgerald received numerous awards and accolades, including multiple Grammy Awards. She was not only celebrated for her vocal prowess but also for her contributions to the cultural landscape of music. She broke racial barriers in the music industry, becoming the first African American woman to win a Grammy Award.

As we celebrate Ella Fitzgerald's life and contributions, we honor not only her legendary talent but also her enduring impact on the world of music. Her music serves as a timeless reminder of the transcendent power of artistry and the universal language of song. Ella Fitzgerald remains an inspiration to countless musicians and a cherished icon in the hearts of music lovers around the world.

Frida Kahlo: Expressing Pain and Resilience Through Art

In the world of art, few figures are as iconic and enigmatic as Frida Kahlo, the Mexican painter known for her striking self-portraits and bold exploration of themes such as pain, identity, and resilience. Her art, characterized by its vivid imagery and emotional depth, continues to captivate audiences and inspire conversations about self-expression and the human experience.

Magdalena Carmen Frida Kahlo y Calderón was born on July 6, 1907, in Coyoacán, a suburb of Mexico City. Her early life was marked by physical challenges, as she contracted polio as a child, which left her with a lifelong limp. However, her life took a dramatic turn when, at the age of 18, she was involved in a near-fatal bus accident that left her with severe injuries, including a fractured spine and pelvis.

Kahlo's recovery from the accident was painful and lengthy, during which she began to explore painting as a form of self-expression and catharsis. Her distinctive style emerged as she used her own image as a recurring subject in her art, often rendered in a surreal and symbolic manner. Her works conveyed both the physical and emotional pain she endured as well as her indomitable spirit.

One of Kahlo's most famous paintings, "The Two Fridas" (1939), is a poignant exploration of her dual identity as a Mexican and as a woman of mixed European and indigenous heritage. In the painting, two versions of Kahlo, one in traditional Mexican attire and the other in Victorian clothing, are depicted holding hands. The painting reflects the complexity of her identity and her deep connection to Mexican culture.

Kahlo's self-portraits are notable not only for their visual impact but also for their emotional depth. They often contain symbolism and allegory, providing glimpses into her inner world. Her art touched on themes such as pain, suffering, love, and the struggle for identity.

Her relationship with fellow artist Diego Rivera, whom she married and divorced, was a central aspect of her life and art. Their turbulent and passionate relationship influenced her work, and Rivera's influence is evident in some of her paintings, where he is portrayed alongside Kahlo.

Kahlo's art was not confined to traditional canvases. She also created a series of "retablos," small paintings on metal sheets, which were often used for religious or votive purposes. Kahlo's retablos, however, were deeply personal, depicting scenes from her life and experiences.

Frida Kahlo's art was celebrated for its unflinching honesty and its exploration of the human condition. She became a symbol of resilience, particularly for women, as she defied societal norms and expectations to pursue her art and express her innermost thoughts and emotions.

Tragically, Kahlo's life was marked by chronic health issues, and she passed away on July 13, 1954, at the age of 47. Her legacy, however, endures through her art, which continues to resonate with audiences worldwide.

In recent years, Frida Kahlo's life and work have experienced a resurgence in popular culture, with exhibitions, films, and books celebrating her contributions to art and her enduring influence on contemporary artists and feminist movements.

As we commemorate Frida Kahlo's contributions to the world of art and her ability to express pain and resilience through her work, we honor her role as a trailblazing artist who challenged conventions and left an indelible mark on the art world.

Aretha Franklin: Becoming the Queen of Soul

In the world of music, few voices have resonated as powerfully and soulfully as that of Aretha Franklin, the legendary American singer known as the "Queen of Soul." Her remarkable vocal talent, emotional depth, and profound influence on the world of music have made her an enduring icon and an inspiration to generations of artists.

Aretha Louise Franklin was born on March 25, 1942, in Memphis, Tennessee. She hailed from a family with deep roots in gospel music, as her father, C.L. Franklin, was a Baptist minister and a prominent gospel singer. Growing up surrounded by the sounds of gospel music, Aretha developed her extraordinary vocal abilities at an early age.

Her journey to becoming the Queen of Soul began in her teenage years when she signed with Columbia Records in 1960. However, it was her move to Atlantic Records in 1966 that marked a turning point in her career. Under the guidance of producer Jerry Wexler, Franklin unleashed her powerhouse voice, combining gospel, R&B, and soul influences to create a groundbreaking sound.

Aretha Franklin's distinctive voice, characterized by its soul-stirring intensity, soaring range, and emotional depth, quickly captured the hearts of listeners worldwide. Her hit singles, including "Respect," "Think," "Chain of Fools," and "Natural Woman," became anthems of empowerment and self-expression during a time of social and cultural change in the United States.

"Respect," in particular, became an anthem of the civil rights and women's rights movements. Franklin's rendition of the song, originally written and recorded by Otis Redding, transformed it into a powerful call for equality and respect. The song's lyrics, "R-E-S-P-E-C-T, find out what it means to me," resonated with audiences far beyond the realm of music.

Throughout her career, Aretha Franklin garnered numerous accolades, including multiple Grammy Awards and recognition as one of the greatest singers of all time. Her performances were marked by their emotional authenticity, often leaving audiences moved to tears or inspired by her unparalleled vocal prowess.

Beyond her success as a singer, Franklin was also a gifted pianist and songwriter. Her ability to infuse her music with personal experiences and emotions added layers of depth to her work.

Aretha Franklin's impact extended beyond the world of music. She was a trailblazer for African American artists and women in the music industry, breaking barriers and achieving mainstream success during a time of racial segregation and gender inequality. Her achievements paved the way for future generations of artists to assert their voices and claim their rightful place in the industry.

Franklin's influence can be heard in the work of countless artists across genres, and her music continues to be celebrated and cherished by listeners of all ages. Her performances, whether on stage or in the recording studio, were electrifying and transcendent, earning her a permanent place in the pantheon of music legends.

Aretha Franklin passed away on August 16, 2018, but her music lives on, reminding us of the power of soulful expression and the enduring impact of a voice that could move mountains and touch hearts.

As we commemorate Aretha Franklin's contributions to the world of music and her indomitable spirit as the Queen of Soul, we honor her role as a trailblazing artist who used her voice to inspire, empower, and create lasting change.

Georgia O'Keeffe: Celebrating the Beauty of the American Landscape

In the world of American art, the name Georgia O'Keeffe stands as a testament to the power of interpretation and a deep connection to the natural world. Her iconic paintings of enlarged flowers, New York skyscrapers, and the Southwestern landscape have left an indelible mark on the art world, celebrating the beauty of the American landscape in unique and captivating ways.

Georgia Totto O'Keeffe was born on November 15, 1887, in Sun Prairie, Wisconsin. From an early age, she displayed a talent and passion for art. Her artistic journey led her to study at the Art Institute of Chicago and later, under the guidance of renowned American modernist Arthur Wesley Dow, at Teachers College, Columbia University.

O'Keeffe's early work was influenced by the principles of abstraction and modernism, reflecting her exposure to avant-garde artistic movements in the early 20th century. However, it was her move to New York City in 1916 that marked a turning point in her career.

In New York, O'Keeffe was introduced to the vibrant artistic circles of the time, including photographer Alfred Stieglitz, who would later become her husband and a significant influence on her art. Under Stieglitz's mentorship and encouragement, O'Keeffe began to explore a distinctive style characterized by bold colors, close-up views of objects, and a focus on the natural world.

One of O'Keeffe's most iconic series of paintings features enlarged flowers, such as her famous "Jimson Weed/White Flower No. 1" (1932). These works, characterized by their attention to detail and vibrant colors, invited viewers to see flowers in a new and intimate way, transcending mere botanical representation to evoke emotion and sensuality.

O'Keeffe's fascination with the American landscape also played a central role in her work. Her visits to New Mexico in the 1920s ignited a deep connection to the Southwestern terrain. The stark deserts, vibrant skies, and unique rock formations of the region became recurring motifs in her art. Her paintings of the American Southwest, such as "Black Mesa Landscape, New Mexico/Out Back of Marie's II" (1930), captured the essence and grandeur of the landscape.

Throughout her career, O'Keeffe's art defied easy categorization, blending elements of modernism, abstraction, and precisionism. Her work encouraged viewers to see the world anew, as she transformed everyday objects and landscapes into evocative and symbolic representations.

Georgia O'Keeffe's influence extended beyond her art. She became a trailblazing figure in the male-dominated art world, challenging conventions and carving out a space for herself as a pioneering female artist. Her impact on American art and culture is immeasurable, as she inspired generations of artists and continues to be celebrated for her innovative vision.

O'Keeffe's work remains a testament to the enduring beauty of the American landscape and the capacity of art to capture its essence. Her paintings invite us to contemplate the world with fresh eyes, to see the extraordinary in the ordinary, and to celebrate the beauty that surrounds us.

Georgia O'Keeffe passed away on March 6, 1986, leaving behind a legacy that continues to inspire and resonate with those who appreciate the transformative power of art and the beauty of the American landscape.

As we commemorate Georgia O'Keeffe's contributions to the world of art and her ability to celebrate the American landscape in all its glory, we honor her role as a trailblazing artist who painted the world as she saw it, and in doing so, invited us to see it anew.

Maria Callas: Redefining Opera with Her Powerful Voice

In the world of opera, the name Maria Callas stands as a towering figure whose extraordinary vocal talent, dramatic intensity, and artistic innovation forever transformed the genre. Often referred to as "La Divina," Callas's powerful voice and dramatic prowess redefined the possibilities of opera and left an indelible mark on the world of classical music.

Maria Callas was born on December 2, 1923, in New York City to Greek immigrant parents. Her early life was marked by her exposure to both American and European cultures, and her love for music became evident at an early age. She began her formal vocal training in Greece and later studied at the prestigious Athens Conservatoire.

Callas's operatic career took off in the late 1940s, and she quickly gained recognition for her exceptional vocal range, precision, and emotional depth. Her powerful soprano voice had a remarkable versatility, enabling her to excel in a wide range of operatic roles, from the bel canto repertoire to the dramatic works of Verdi and Puccini.

One of the defining aspects of Callas's artistry was her dedication to character portrayal and dramatic interpretation. She believed that opera was not merely about vocal acrobatics but also about conveying the emotions and complexities of the characters she portrayed on stage. Her commitment to dramatic authenticity elevated opera to new heights.

Callas's partnership with Italian conductor Tullio Serafin and her collaborations with renowned stage directors, such as Luchino Visconti, contributed to her reputation as a trailblazer in the world of opera. Her interpretations of iconic roles, including Norma, Tosca, and Medea, were marked by their emotional intensity and dramatic depth.

One of Callas's most celebrated achievements was her revival of the bel canto repertoire, particularly the works of Vincenzo Bellini and Gaetano Donizetti. Her performances in roles like Norma and Lucia di Lammermoor showcased her exceptional vocal agility and control, reviving interest in these operas and influencing subsequent generations of singers.

Callas's personal life was often as dramatic as the roles she portrayed on stage. Her tumultuous relationship with Greek shipping magnate Aristotle Onassis and her struggles with weight fluctuations and vocal health were widely covered by the media. Despite these challenges, her artistic commitment remained unwavering.

In 1957, Callas made her historic debut at Milan's La Scala opera house, a performance that solidified her status as an opera legend. Her interpretations of iconic operas, such as "Tosca" and "La Traviata," became legendary and continue to be cherished by opera enthusiasts.

However, by the mid-1960s, vocal challenges and personal difficulties led to a decline in Callas's stage appearances. She withdrew from performing but remained active as a recording artist, leaving behind a rich legacy of studio recordings that showcase her vocal prowess and interpretive skills.

Maria Callas passed away on September 16, 1977, but her influence on the world of opera endures. Her contributions to the art form are celebrated for their technical brilliance, emotional depth, and commitment to dramatic truth. She remains an inspiration to opera singers and enthusiasts worldwide.

As we commemorate Maria Callas's contributions to the world of opera and her ability to redefine the genre with her powerful voice and dramatic artistry, we honor her role as a trailblazing artist who left an indelible mark on the world of classical music.

Chapter 6: Influential Women in Humanitarian Work

Faye Wattleton: A Trailblazer in Reproductive Rights Advocacy

Faye Wattleton, a pioneering advocate for reproductive rights and women's health, has made an indelible mark on the landscape of reproductive rights advocacy in the United States. Serving as the President of Planned Parenthood Federation of America, she led transformative efforts to expand access to reproductive healthcare and comprehensive sex education, leaving a lasting impact on the field.

Wattleton's leadership at Planned Parenthood was characterized by her unwavering commitment to women's health and reproductive autonomy. Under her guidance, the organization played a vital role in advocating for the rights of individuals to make informed choices about their reproductive health, including access to contraception and safe, legal abortion.

One of the defining aspects of Faye Wattleton's tenure was her dedication to ensuring that reproductive healthcare and education were accessible to all, regardless of socioeconomic status, geography, or background. Her work focused on breaking down barriers to access, advocating for policies that expanded healthcare options, and promoting comprehensive sex education to empower individuals with knowledge and agency over their own bodies.

Wattleton's advocacy extended far beyond the walls of Planned Parenthood. She used her platform to engage in meaningful dialogues about reproductive rights, challenging societal stigmas and advocating for the destigmatization of reproductive healthcare. Her commitment to open and honest conversations about sexuality and reproductive health paved the way for greater awareness and understanding.

Throughout her career, Faye Wattleton received numerous accolades and awards for her contributions to reproductive rights advocacy. Her legacy continues to inspire generations of activists and healthcare providers who are dedicated to preserving and advancing the rights of individuals to make choices about their own bodies.

As we celebrate Faye Wattleton's life and work, we honor not only her groundbreaking leadership at Planned Parenthood but also her enduring legacy as a champion of reproductive rights and women's health. Her advocacy reminds us of the importance of access to comprehensive healthcare and education, as well as the ongoing fight to protect and expand reproductive autonomy for all. Faye Wattleton stands as a trailblazer in the quest for reproductive justice, leaving behind a legacy that continues to shape the conversation surrounding reproductive rights and healthcare.

Shirin Ebadi: Championing Human Rights and Justice in Iran

Shirin Ebadi, an Iranian lawyer and Nobel Peace Prize laureate, stands as an unwavering advocate for human rights, particularly those of women, children, and political prisoners in Iran. Born in 1947 in Hamadan, Iran, her courageous efforts have shone a spotlight on human rights abuses and injustice, making her a symbol of resistance and justice in her homeland and beyond.

At the core of Shirin Ebadi's remarkable legacy is her unyielding commitment to defending the rights and dignity of the most vulnerable in society. Throughout her career as a lawyer and activist, she has fearlessly championed the cause of women's rights, advocating for gender equality, access to education, and protection from domestic violence and discrimination.

Ebadi's advocacy extends to the rights of children, particularly those who face exploitation, abuse, and neglect. Her work has focused on improving the legal and social framework to ensure a safer and more equitable environment for the youngest members of society.

One of the defining aspects of Ebadi's activism is her tireless dedication to political prisoners and those unjustly detained. She has consistently raised her voice against the violation of due process and the abuse of power in Iran's legal system, advocating for the release of those imprisoned for their beliefs or political activities.

In 2003, Shirin Ebadi was awarded the Nobel Peace Prize for her courageous efforts in advancing human rights in Iran. Her recognition on the global stage brought attention to the challenges faced by activists and advocates in the region, as well as the importance of upholding universal human rights principles.

Despite facing threats to her own safety and well-being, Ebadi has continued to be a beacon of hope for those seeking justice and accountability. Her resilience in the face of adversity serves as an inspiration to human rights defenders worldwide.

As we celebrate Shirin Ebadi's life and contributions, we honor not only her unwavering advocacy for human rights but also her enduring legacy as a symbol of resistance and justice. Her courageous efforts remind us of the transformative power of individuals who stand up for the rights and dignity of others, even in the most challenging of circumstances. Shirin Ebadi remains a steadfast voice for the voiceless and a beacon of hope for those who strive for a more just and equitable world.

Mother Teresa: Devoting Her Life to the Poorest of the Poor

In the annals of humanitarian work, few names evoke as much reverence and admiration as that of Mother Teresa, the Albanian-born nun who dedicated her life to serving the most destitute and marginalized individuals on the streets of Kolkata, India. Her unwavering commitment to compassion, care, and selflessness made her a global symbol of love and service.

Born as Anjezë Gonxhe Bojaxhiu on August 26, 1910, in Skopje, which is now part of North Macedonia, Mother Teresa's early life was marked by a profound sense of faith and a desire to help those in need. At the age of 18, she left her family to join the Sisters of Loreto, an Irish Catholic missionary order, and took the name Sister Mary Teresa.

Mother Teresa's journey to India in 1929 marked the beginning of her lifelong mission to serve the poor. For nearly two decades, she taught at St. Mary's School in Kolkata, but her desire to help the impoverished and suffering people she encountered in the city compelled her to take a more direct and hands-on approach to humanitarian work.

In 1950, Mother Teresa founded the Missionaries of Charity, a congregation dedicated to the service of "the poorest of the poor." The organization's mission was to provide food, shelter, medical care, and, above all, love to those who were suffering and abandoned on the streets of Kolkata.

Under Mother Teresa's leadership, the Missionaries of Charity expanded their efforts beyond Kolkata, establishing centers and homes for the needy across India and eventually in other countries around the world. Her tireless work addressed the needs of the sick, the dying, orphaned children, and those living in extreme poverty.

One of the most iconic aspects of Mother Teresa's work was the care she provided to the terminally ill and the dying. She believed that every person, regardless of their circumstances, deserved dignity and compassion in their final moments. Her Home for the Dying, also known as Kalighat, became a place of solace and comfort for those who had been abandoned by society.

Mother Teresa's approach to humanitarian work was marked by her humility and willingness to personally serve those in need. She often visited the slums of Kolkata, carrying the sick and destitute to her centers, cleaning their wounds, and offering them solace. Her simple white sari with blue stripes became an iconic symbol of her dedication.

Her work did not go unnoticed, and she received numerous awards and honors, including the Nobel Peace Prize in 1979. However, she remained focused on her mission and continued to serve the poorest of the poor with unwavering dedication.

Mother Teresa passed away on September 5, 1997, but her legacy lives on through the Missionaries of Charity and the countless individuals she inspired to engage in acts of love and service. Her life and work serve as a reminder of the profound impact one person can have in alleviating suffering and bringing hope to the most vulnerable.

As we commemorate Mother Teresa's contributions to humanitarian work and her lifelong devotion to the poorest of the poor, we honor her role as a trailblazing figure who exemplified the true meaning of compassion, selflessness, and love for humanity.

Clara Barton: Founding the American Red Cross

In the annals of humanitarian history, Clara Barton's name stands as a symbol of compassion, resilience, and unwavering dedication to the relief of human suffering. Her pioneering efforts in establishing the American Red Cross, her tireless work during the Civil War, and her advocacy for humanitarian causes left an indelible mark on the field of humanitarian work.

Clarissa "Clara" Harlowe Barton was born on December 25, 1821, in North Oxford, Massachusetts. From a young age, she displayed a deep sense of empathy and a desire to help those in need. Her early career path included teaching, but her true calling as a humanitarian emerged during the American Civil War.

During the Civil War, Clara Barton volunteered as a nurse, providing care and comfort to wounded soldiers on both sides of the conflict. Her courage and dedication were evident as she ventured close to the front lines, often in the midst of battles, to tend to the wounded and provide medical supplies.

One of Barton's most significant contributions during the war was her work in establishing a system for tracking and identifying missing soldiers. She diligently corresponded with families and recorded information about the fallen and missing, earning her the nickname "Angel of the Battlefield."

After the Civil War, Barton's commitment to humanitarian work continued to grow. Inspired by her experiences in Europe and the work of the International Red Cross, she founded the American Red Cross in 1881. Her vision was to establish an organization that would provide aid to those affected by disasters, armed conflicts, and public health emergencies.

Under Barton's leadership, the American Red Cross initially focused on disaster response and relief efforts. The organization played a pivotal role in providing relief to victims of natural disasters, including hurricanes and floods. Barton's tireless advocacy also led to the United States becoming a signatory to the Geneva Convention, which extended protections to wounded soldiers and established principles of humanitarian law during armed conflicts.

Barton's leadership of the American Red Cross expanded its scope to include support for military personnel and veterans. She tirelessly worked to locate missing soldiers, provide aid to their families, and advocate for the rights of veterans.

Clara Barton's humanitarian efforts extended beyond U.S. borders as well. She played a critical role in the relief efforts during the Franco-Prussian War and the relief for victims of the Armenian massacres in the 1890s. Her commitment to alleviating human suffering knew no geographical boundaries.

Clara Barton passed away on April 12, 1912, but her legacy lives on through the American Red Cross, which continues to provide humanitarian aid and disaster relief both nationally and internationally. Her pioneering spirit, dedication to the welfare of others, and belief in the power of collective action remain central tenets of the organization she founded.

As we commemorate Clara Barton's contributions to humanitarian work and her founding of the American Red Cross, we honor her role as a trailblazing figure who transformed the landscape of humanitarian assistance and left an enduring legacy of compassion and service.

Eleanor Roosevelt: Championing Human Rights at the United Nations

In the land of global human rights advocacy and diplomacy, few figures have left as profound an impact as Eleanor Roosevelt. Her tireless commitment to championing human rights and her pivotal role in the establishment of the Universal Declaration of Human Rights at the United Nations have made her an enduring symbol of moral leadership and social justice.

Anna Eleanor Roosevelt was born on October 11, 1884, in New York City. She came from a privileged background but was deeply influenced by the values of empathy, social responsibility, and advocacy instilled by her parents. Her marriage to Franklin D. Roosevelt, who later became the 32nd President of the United States, marked the beginning of her public life and her journey as an advocate for social and political change.

Eleanor Roosevelt's tenure as First Lady from 1933 to 1945 was marked by her active engagement in public affairs. She redefined the role of First Lady, using her platform to advocate for civil rights, women's rights, and economic and social justice. She conducted press conferences, wrote a syndicated newspaper column, and traveled extensively to learn about the conditions of ordinary Americans during the Great Depression.

One of Eleanor Roosevelt's most enduring legacies was her dedication to civil rights and racial equality. She was an outspoken critic of segregation and discrimination and worked to advance the civil rights agenda during a time when such advocacy was met with resistance and hostility. Her support for the Tuskegee Airmen, African American aviators in World War II, and her resignation from the Daughters of the American Revolution (DAR) when they denied African American singer Marian Anderson the use of Constitution Hall highlighted her commitment to racial justice.

Eleanor Roosevelt's influence extended beyond her role as First Lady. After World War II, she became a delegate to the United Nations General Assembly and was appointed as the chair of the United Nations Commission on Human Rights. In this role, she played a central part in drafting the Universal Declaration of Human Rights, which was adopted by the United Nations in 1948.

The Universal Declaration of Human Rights is a foundational document that outlines the fundamental rights and freedoms to which all individuals are entitled, regardless of their background or nationality. Eleanor Roosevelt's leadership and diplomacy were instrumental in bridging differences among nations and ensuring the declaration's adoption.

Throughout her life, Eleanor Roosevelt continued to advocate for human rights, social justice, and the empowerment of marginalized communities. Her work was marked by her deep empathy for the suffering and oppressed and her belief in the power of international cooperation to address global challenges.

Eleanor Roosevelt passed away on November 7, 1962, but her legacy endures. Her contributions to human rights and her role in shaping the Universal Declaration of Human Rights have left an indelible mark on the world. The declaration remains a cornerstone of international human rights law and a testament to her unwavering commitment to the dignity and worth of every individual.

As we commemorate Eleanor Roosevelt's advocacy for human rights and her pivotal role in the United Nations, we honor her as a trailblazing figure who exemplified the values of empathy, justice, and the belief that human rights are the birthright of all people.

Chapter 7: Groundbreaking Women in Technology

Marie Stopes: A Trailblazer in Women's Reproductive Rights and Family Planning

Marie Stopes, a pioneering figure in the field of birth control and women's reproductive rights, made enduring contributions that have had a profound impact on women's health and autonomy. Her legacy is marked by her relentless advocacy, groundbreaking research, and the establishment of the first birth control clinic in the United Kingdom.

At the heart of Marie Stopes' remarkable legacy is her unwavering commitment to expanding access to birth control and family planning. In an era when discussions about contraception were often shrouded in stigma and misinformation, she emerged as a vocal advocate for women's right to control their reproductive destinies.

In 1921, Stopes founded the first birth control clinic in the United Kingdom, known as the Mother's Clinic, which later became the Marie Stopes International organization. This groundbreaking initiative provided women with access to contraception and reproductive healthcare services, empowering them to make informed choices about their family planning.

Marie Stopes' advocacy extended to her prolific research in the field of birth control and contraception methods. Her work contributed significantly to the development and understanding of contraceptive techniques, leading to advancements that have improved the lives of countless individuals and families worldwide.

Throughout her career, Stopes faced significant opposition and controversy due to her advocacy for birth control and family planning. However, her unwavering dedication to women's reproductive rights and health ultimately prevailed, laying the foundation for the modern reproductive justice movement.

Marie Stopes' enduring impact on women's health and autonomy is felt to this day. Her pioneering efforts paved the way for the widespread availability of contraception and family planning services, enabling individuals to make choices that align with their life goals and circumstances.

As we celebrate Marie Stopes' life and contributions, we honor not only her groundbreaking work in the field of birth control but also her enduring legacy as a champion of women's reproductive rights. Her advocacy reminds us of the importance of choice, education, and access to reproductive healthcare, as well as the ongoing fight for gender equality and bodily autonomy. Marie Stopes continues to inspire and empower individuals to take control of their reproductive destinies, making her a true trailblazer in the realm of women's health and rights.

Ada Lovelace: Pioneering Computer Programming

In the space of technology and computer science, the name Ada Lovelace shines as a beacon of innovation and foresight. Often recognized as the world's first computer programmer, Ada Lovelace's visionary work laid the foundation for modern computer programming and artificial intelligence.

Augusta Ada King, Countess of Lovelace, was born on December 10, 1815, in London, England. She was the daughter of the poet Lord Byron, but it was her mother, Anne Isabella Milbanke, who played a significant role in Ada's education and intellectual development. Ada was introduced to mathematics and science from a young age, reflecting her mother's belief that these subjects could provide a counterbalance to her father's artistic temperament.

Ada's intellectual curiosity and aptitude for mathematics became evident early on. Her education was guided by prominent mathematicians and scientists of the time, including Mary Somerville and Charles Babbage. Babbage, often considered the "father of the computer," designed the Analytical Engine, a mechanical, general-purpose computing device that was never built during his lifetime.

It was Ada Lovelace's collaboration with Charles Babbage that would lead to her groundbreaking contributions to the field of computer science. In the

1840s, she translated an article about Babbage's Analytical Engine written by the Italian mathematician Luigi Federico Menabrea. In the process of translation, Lovelace added extensive notes and annotations that went beyond mere translation.

Ada Lovelace's notes, often referred to as "Notes on the Analytical Engine," are where her pioneering ideas in computer programming emerge. In these notes, she articulated the concept of "Bernoulli numbers," which she saw as a potential application of the Analytical Engine. Importantly, Lovelace understood that the engine could be programmed to perform operations beyond mathematical calculations, including creating music and generating art—a visionary insight into the potential of computing that was well ahead of its time.

What set Lovelace's work apart was her recognition that the Analytical Engine had the capacity for "weaving algebraic patterns," making her the first person to realize that a machine could be programmed to perform tasks beyond pure mathematical calculation. Her notes contained an algorithm for calculating Bernoulli numbers, which is now considered the world's first computer program. This algorithm is often regarded as the first instance of a computer program designed to be carried out by a machine, a fundamental concept in modern computer science.

Although the Analytical Engine was never constructed during Ada Lovelace's lifetime, her visionary ideas laid the conceptual groundwork for the development of modern computers and computer programming. Her work remained relatively obscure until the mid-20th century when her contributions were rediscovered and recognized as pioneering.

Ada Lovelace passed away on November 27, 1852, at the young age of 36. Her legacy, however, endures in the world of technology and computer science. The computer programming language "Ada," developed for the United States Department of Defense, was named in her honor, and the second Tuesday in October is celebrated as Ada Lovelace Day, a global event that highlights the achievements of women in science, technology, engineering, and mathematics (STEM).

As we commemorate Ada Lovelace's groundbreaking contributions to computer programming and her visionary insights into the possibilities of computing, we honor her role as a trailblazing figure who foresaw the transformative impact of technology on the world.

Grace Hopper: Innovating in Computer Science and the Navy

In the annals of computer science and technology, the name Grace Hopper stands as a symbol of innovation, persistence, and trailblazing contributions. Often referred to as "Amazing Grace," Hopper was a pioneer in the field of computer programming, and her work laid the foundation for modern computing and software development.

Grace Brewster Murray Hopper was born on December 9, 1906, in New York City. From an early age, she displayed an aptitude for mathematics and an inquisitive mind. She pursued her education at Vassar College, where she earned a bachelor's degree in mathematics and physics in 1928. She then went on to earn a master's degree in mathematics from Yale University in 1930.

Hopper's career took an unexpected turn when she decided to enlist in the United States Navy during World War II. Her exceptional mathematical and analytical skills led to her assignment to the Bureau of Ordnance's Computation Project at Harvard University, where she worked on the Harvard Mark I, one of the earliest electromechanical computers.

Hopper's work with the Mark I marked the beginning of her influential career in computer science. She developed the first-ever compiler, known as the "A-0 System," which allowed programmers to write code in a more human-readable format. This innovation laid the foundation for modern computer programming languages and made it possible to write software that could be used on multiple computer systems.

One of Hopper's most enduring contributions was the development of COBOL (Common Business-Oriented Language), a high-level programming language designed for business and administrative applications. COBOL simplified programming and made it accessible to a broader range of users. Its adoption revolutionized the software industry and enabled the development of software that could run on different computer systems without major modifications.

Hopper's career in the Navy spanned three decades, during which she attained the rank of rear admiral. She continued to work on cutting-edge computing projects, including the development of the UNIVAC I, one of the earliest commercially produced computers.

After retiring from the Navy in 1986, Grace Hopper remained active in the computing community. She received numerous awards and honors during her lifetime, including the National Medal of Technology and the Presidential Medal of Freedom. Her commitment to education and the advancement of women in technology also left a lasting legacy.

Grace Hopper passed away on January 1, 1992, but her influence endures in the world of computer science and technology. The Grace Hopper Celebration of Women in Computing, an annual conference, honors her contributions and supports women pursuing careers in technology.

As we commemorate Grace Hopper's groundbreaking innovations in computer science and her pioneering role in making computing accessible and user-friendly, we honor her as a trailblazing figure who reshaped the landscape of technology and programming.

Hedy Lamarr: Inventing Frequency-Hopping Spread Spectrum Technology

In the world of technology and telecommunications, the name Hedy Lamarr shines as a testament to the power of innovation, intellect, and the relentless pursuit of scientific advancement. While renowned as a Hollywood actress, Lamarr's groundbreaking invention of frequency-hopping spread spectrum technology has left an enduring mark on modern communication systems.

Hedwig Eva Maria Kiesler was born on November 9, 1914, in Vienna, Austria. From a young age, she displayed a keen interest in science and engineering, influenced by her father, who was a successful banker with a passion for invention. This early exposure to innovation and her own curiosity about the world would later play a crucial role in her life.

In the late 1930s, Hedy Kiesler married Friedrich Mandl, an Austrian munitions manufacturer and arms dealer. Mandl's involvement in the defense industry exposed Hedy to discussions about military technology and weaponry. It was during these conversations that she gleaned valuable insights into the world of wireless communication and radio-controlled torpedoes, which would later inspire her groundbreaking invention.

Escaping an oppressive marriage, Hedy fled to the United States in 1937. It was there, amidst the glamour of Hollywood, that she adopted the screen name "Hedy Lamarr" and pursued a successful career as an actress, becoming a celebrated Hollywood star. However, her passion for science and invention never waned.

During World War II, Lamarr's concern for the Allied forces led her to collaborate with composer and inventor George Antheil. Together, they developed a groundbreaking technology known as frequency-hopping spread spectrum. This innovation aimed to address the problem of radio-controlled torpedoes being jammed or intercepted by enemy forces.

Frequency-hopping spread spectrum involved rapidly and randomly changing the frequency of radio signals used to transmit information. This method made it extremely difficult for adversaries to jam or intercept the signals, as they could not predict the changing frequencies. The concept was ahead of its time and formed the basis for modern technologies such as Bluetooth, Wi-Fi, and secure military communication systems.

In 1942, Lamarr and Antheil were granted a patent for their frequency-hopping spread spectrum invention. However, it wasn't until many years later that the significance of their work was fully recognized and embraced by the telecommunications industry.

Hedy Lamarr's invention laid the groundwork for secure and resilient wireless communication systems that are now integral to our everyday lives. Her pioneering work in technology is celebrated as a precursor to the digital age and the modern wireless world.

Despite the initial lack of recognition, Hedy Lamarr's contribution to science and technology has received numerous posthumous honors and awards. She is remembered not only for her captivating presence on the silver screen but also for her brilliant mind and her lasting impact on the world of telecommunications.

Hedy Lamarr passed away on January 19, 2000, but her legacy as a trailblazing inventor continues to inspire scientists, engineers, and innovators to push the boundaries of what is possible in the realm of technology and communication.

As we commemorate Hedy Lamarr's pioneering invention of frequency-hopping spread spectrum technology and her enduring impact on modern communication systems, we honor her as a trailblazing figure who bridged the worlds of Hollywood and science, leaving a legacy that continues to shape our connected world.

Sheryl Sandberg: Promoting Gender Equality in Silicon Valley

In the contemporary landscape of technology and business, Sheryl Sandberg stands as a prominent figure who has made significant strides in promoting gender equality and empowering women in the tech industry. As the Chief Operating Officer of Facebook and an influential author and speaker, Sandberg's advocacy for women's rights and her leadership in Silicon Valley have reshaped the conversation around diversity and inclusion.

Sheryl Kara Sandberg was born on August 28, 1969, in Washington, D.C. Her academic prowess and leadership abilities were evident from a young age, and she went on to earn a bachelor's degree in economics from Harvard University and an MBA from Harvard Business School.

After completing her education, Sandberg embarked on a diverse career that included roles at the World Bank, McKinsey & Company, and Google. It was during her tenure at Google that she gained recognition for her contributions to the company's advertising and online sales efforts. This experience paved the way for her transition to Facebook in 2008 when she joined as Chief Operating Officer.

At Facebook, Sandberg played a pivotal role in driving the company's growth and success. Her leadership was instrumental in scaling Facebook's operations, monetizing its platform, and expanding its global reach. Under her guidance, Facebook transformed into one of the most influential and profitable technology companies in the world.

However, it was outside her role as COO that Sheryl Sandberg made an even more significant impact. In 2010, she gave a TED Talk titled "Why We Have Too Few Women Leaders," which sparked a global conversation about the underrepresentation of women in leadership positions across various industries. Sandberg's candid and insightful observations resonated with countless women and inspired her to write the best-selling book "Lean In: Women, Work, and the Will to Lead."

"Lean In" became a manifesto for women's empowerment in the workplace, encouraging women to pursue their career ambitions, assert themselves in leadership roles, and challenge gender biases. The book also prompted the creation of LeanIn.org, a nonprofit organization focused on supporting women's career advancement and promoting gender equality.

Sheryl Sandberg's commitment to gender diversity and inclusion extended beyond the pages of her book. She advocated for the importance of male allies in the fight for gender equality and initiated campaigns like "Ban Bossy" to encourage girls to embrace leadership roles.

In addition to her advocacy for women's rights, Sandberg faced personal challenges when her husband, Dave Goldberg, passed away unexpectedly in 2015. Her resilience and openness about her grief sparked conversations about the importance of resilience and community support during times of adversity.

Sheryl Sandberg's work and influence have had a profound impact on the technology industry and corporate culture as a whole. She has been recognized for her leadership and advocacy, including her inclusion in TIME magazine's list of the 100 most influential people in the world.

As we commemorate Sheryl Sandberg's tireless efforts to promote gender equality and empower women in the tech industry and beyond, we honor her as a trailblazing figure who continues to inspire individuals and organizations to work towards a more equitable and inclusive future.

Chapter 8: Female Explorers and Adventurers

Mae C. Jemison: Breaking Barriers and Shaping the Future of Space Exploration

Mae C. Jemison, an astronaut and trailblazer, etched her name in history as the first African American woman to journey into space. Born in Decatur, Alabama, in 1956, her remarkable achievements have made her not only an icon of space exploration but also a symbol of diversity and inclusion in STEM (science, technology, engineering, and mathematics) fields.

At the core of Mae C. Jemison's legacy is her groundbreaking journey into space. In 1992, aboard the Space Shuttle Endeavour, she made history as the first African American woman to travel beyond Earth's atmosphere, demonstrating that the boundaries of possibility in space exploration are not limited by gender or race.

Jemison's accomplishments inspire and resonate with future generations of scientists, astronauts, and dreamers. Her achievement serves as a testament to the power of perseverance, determination, and a pioneering spirit. She shattered not only the glass ceiling but also the outer limits of Earth's atmosphere, proving that the cosmos belong to all of humanity.

Beyond her historic spaceflight, Mae C. Jemison has been a tireless advocate for diversity in STEM fields. She has used her platform to encourage underrepresented communities, especially young girls and minorities, to pursue careers in science and space exploration. Her commitment to inclusion underscores the importance of diverse perspectives in advancing human knowledge and solving the challenges of the future.

Jemison's legacy is a source of inspiration for individuals of all backgrounds who aspire to reach for the stars, both figuratively and literally. Her achievements serve as a reminder that the frontiers of science and space are open to anyone with the courage to dream and the determination to pursue those dreams.

As we celebrate Mae C. Jemison's life and contributions, we honor not only her historic journey into space but also her enduring impact as a role model and advocate for diversity in STEM. Her legacy reminds us that the cosmos are a shared frontier, waiting for the next generation of explorers to push the boundaries of human knowledge and to reach for the stars. Mae C. Jemison's name will forever be synonymous with the idea that no dream is too big, and no challenge is insurmountable.

Amelia Earhart: Breaking Barriers in Aviation

In the space of aviation and exploration, the name Amelia Earhart is synonymous with courage, determination, and a relentless pursuit of dreams. Her groundbreaking achievements in aviation, along with her adventurous spirit, made her an iconic figure and a trailblazer for women in the field.

Amelia Mary Earhart was born on July 24, 1897, in Atchison, Kansas, USA. Her fascination with flight was sparked at an early age when she saw her first airplane at a county fair. This encounter ignited a passion for aviation that would shape her life and career.

Amelia's journey into aviation began in 1920 when she took her first flying lesson, eventually earning her pilot's license. Her fearless pursuit of flight led her to become one of the first female aviators to set numerous records and achieve remarkable milestones.

In 1928, Amelia Earhart became the first woman to fly across the Atlantic Ocean as a passenger, earning her instant acclaim and recognition. However, she was not content with merely being a passenger; she aspired to be a pioneer in her own right.

In 1932, Amelia achieved a historic milestone by becoming the first woman to solo across the Atlantic, completing the journey in just under 15 hours. Her determination and courage in the face of adversity were evident as she navigated through challenging weather conditions and technical difficulties.

Amelia Earhart's list of accomplishments continued to grow. In 1935, she became the first person, male or female, to fly solo from Hawaii to California, a remarkable feat considering the vast expanse of the Pacific Ocean. Her daring spirit and commitment to pushing the boundaries of flight captivated the world.

Amelia's most ambitious adventure came in 1937 when she embarked on an around-the-world flight. Tragically, her plane disappeared somewhere over the Pacific Ocean, and despite extensive search efforts, she and her navigator, Fred Noonan, were never found. Their disappearance remains one of the greatest mysteries in aviation history.

Although her life was cut short, Amelia Earhart's legacy endures. Her achievements shattered gender stereotypes in aviation and paved the way for future generations of female pilots and explorers. She inspired countless women to pursue careers in aviation and adventure, demonstrating that the sky was not the limit for their aspirations.

Amelia Earhart's legacy is not confined to her feats in the air; she also left a lasting impact on the world's understanding of aviation and exploration. Her life and achievements remind us that dreams, courage, and determination can lead to extraordinary accomplishments.

As we commemorate Amelia Earhart's groundbreaking achievements in aviation and her enduring legacy as a symbol of courage and ambition, we honor her as a trailblazing figure who soared to new heights, leaving an indelible mark on the world of exploration.

Sacagawea: Guiding the Lewis and Clark Expedition

In the annals of American exploration and the opening of the West, the name Sacagawea stands as a symbol of resilience, resourcefulness, and invaluable guidance. As a young Shoshone woman, she played a pivotal role in the success of the Lewis and Clark expedition, which is often regarded as one of the greatest exploratory endeavors in American history.

Sacagawea was born in the Lemhi Valley of present-day Idaho around 1788. Her early life was marked by the dramatic upheavals of European contact and

Native American life in the American West. At the tender age of 12 or 13, she found herself thrust into a pivotal moment in history.

In 1804, Meriwether Lewis and William Clark embarked on an epic expedition, known as the Corps of Discovery, to explore the newly acquired Louisiana Purchase and find a route to the Pacific Ocean. They recognized the need for an interpreter and guide who could navigate the diverse landscapes and Native American tribes they would encounter.

Sacagawea's journey with Lewis and Clark began in 1805 when she, along with her husband Toussaint Charbonneau, a French-Canadian fur trapper, joined the expedition. Sacagawea's knowledge of the Shoshone language and her familiarity with the terrain made her an invaluable asset to the team.

One of the most famous episodes in Sacagawea's role as a guide occurred in the spring of 1805. The expedition encountered the Shoshone tribe, and Sacagawea was able to communicate with her brother Cameahwait, who was the chief. Her reunion with her people and the acquisition of horses from the Shoshone were pivotal moments that enabled the expedition to continue its westward journey.

Throughout the expedition, Sacagawea's presence had a profound impact on interactions with Native American tribes they encountered. Her status as a young mother also served to dispel any potential hostilities, as the sight of a woman and her infant was seen as a symbol of peace.

Sacagawea's contributions extended beyond her role as an interpreter and guide. She foraged for edible plants, served as a source of cultural knowledge, and was a symbol of unity and diplomacy. Her presence was a testament to the resilience and adaptability of Native American women in the face of challenging circumstances.

The Lewis and Clark expedition reached the Pacific Ocean in November 1805 and returned to St. Louis in September 1806, having accomplished its mission of mapping and exploring the newly acquired territory. Sacagawea's guidance and resourcefulness were crucial to the expedition's success.

After the journey, Sacagawea's life remains somewhat shrouded in mystery. It is believed that she passed away around 1812, but her legacy endures. Her contributions to American exploration are commemorated in numerous ways, including the naming of mountain peaks, rivers, and even a U.S. coin in her honor.

Sacagawea's story serves as a powerful reminder of the often-overlooked roles played by Indigenous women in shaping American history. Her resilience, adaptability, and cultural knowledge were essential in the unfolding of a historic expedition that expanded the horizons of the young nation.

As we commemorate Sacagawea's vital role in guiding the Lewis and Clark expedition and her enduring legacy as a symbol of Indigenous wisdom and strength, we honor her as a trailblazing figure who contributed significantly to the exploration and understanding of the American West.

Nellie Bly: Circumnavigating the Globe in Record Time

In the world of intrepid journalism and daring adventures, the name Nellie Bly shines as a beacon of audacity and determination. Her remarkable journey to circumnavigate the globe in record time, as a pioneering female journalist in the late 19th century, is a testament to her unyielding spirit and commitment to breaking boundaries.

Born as Elizabeth Jane Cochran on May 5, 1864, in Cochran's Mills, Pennsylvania, she adopted the pen name "Nellie Bly" when she began her career as a journalist. At a time when few opportunities existed for women in the field of journalism, Bly's tenacity and talent propelled her into the spotlight.

Nellie Bly gained widespread recognition for her daring investigative reporting, particularly her expose on the deplorable conditions at the Women's Lunatic Asylum on Blackwell's Island in New York City. Her undercover reporting, which involved feigning insanity to gain admission to the asylum, resulted in a series of articles that led to significant reforms in the treatment of the mentally ill.

In 1889, Nellie Bly embarked on her most audacious adventure yet—the race to circumnavigate the globe in less than 80 days, inspired by Jules Verne's novel "Around the World in Eighty Days." Bly's journey was not only a test of speed but also a groundbreaking feat of journalism.

Setting off from New York City on November 14, 1889, Nellie Bly traveled by steamship, train, rickshaw, and even mule, crossing continents and oceans. Her dispatches from the road were eagerly awaited by readers, who followed her progress with bated breath. She reported on the people she met, the cultures she encountered, and the challenges she faced, all while racing against the clock.

Bly's relentless pace and determination paid off when she arrived back in New York City on January 25, 1890, just 72 days after her departure. Her achievement not only shattered the fictional record set by Phileas Fogg but also set a real-world record for the fastest circumnavigation of the globe by any means.

Nellie Bly's triumphant return to New York was met with jubilation and acclaim. Her journey had captured the imagination of the public and had demonstrated the capabilities of a determined and fearless female journalist. Her record-breaking adventure became a symbol of women's ability to excel in traditionally male-dominated fields.

Following her globe-trotting feat, Nellie Bly continued her career in journalism, writing for various publications and advocating for social causes, including women's suffrage. Her fearless reporting and commitment to social justice left an indelible mark on the field of investigative journalism.

Nellie Bly's legacy endures as an inspiration to journalists, adventurers, and women pursuing their ambitions. Her willingness to push the boundaries of what was considered possible, combined with her dedication to social reform, solidify her place in history as a trailblazing figure who fearlessly navigated uncharted territory.

As we commemorate Nellie Bly's audacious journey around the globe in record time and her pioneering contributions to investigative journalism, we honor her as a trailblazing adventurer and journalist who blazed a trail for future generations of women in media and exploration.

Gertrude Bell: Mapping and Exploring the Middle East

Gertrude Bell emerges as a remarkable figure whose contributions in mapping and exploring the Middle East, particularly during the early 20th century, shaped the geopolitical landscape of the region and left an indelible mark on history.

Gertrude Margaret Lowthian Bell was born on July 14, 1868, in Washington Hall, County Durham, England. From a young age, she displayed a thirst for knowledge, a love of languages, and an adventurous spirit. Her upbringing afforded her access to education and culture, instilling in her a deep appreciation for the diverse cultures of the world.

Bell's journey into the Middle East began in the late 19th century when she embarked on a series of travels to the region. Her curiosity and fascination with the Arabian desert, its people, and its history would become the driving force behind her explorations.

One of Bell's most significant contributions was her extensive work in mapping and surveying the Arabian desert, which included travels through present-day Iraq, Jordan, Syria, and Saudi Arabia. Her meticulous surveying efforts produced maps that were not only highly accurate but also invaluable for future exploration, archaeology, and military operations in the region.

Bell's explorations extended beyond geography. She immersed herself in the cultures and languages of the Middle East, becoming fluent in Arabic, Persian, and Turkish. Her deep understanding of the region's history and politics made her a trusted advisor to British officials and diplomats during a critical period of colonialism and nation-building.

During World War I, Gertrude Bell served the British government as an intelligence officer, where her knowledge of the Middle East was invaluable. She played a key role in the Arab Revolt against the Ottoman Empire and in the negotiations that followed the war, including the drawing of borders and the establishment of new nations in the aftermath of the conflict.

Bell's influence extended to her role in shaping the modern state of Iraq. Her close collaboration with King Faisal I and her expertise in regional dynamics contributed to the establishment of Iraq as a sovereign nation. She even played a role in selecting Baghdad as the country's capital.

In addition to her diplomatic and political endeavors, Gertrude Bell was an accomplished writer and archaeologist. She documented her travels and experiences in books, articles, and letters, providing valuable insights into the cultures, landscapes, and history of the Middle East.

Gertrude Bell's life and contributions were cut short when she passed away on July 12, 1926, in Baghdad, Iraq. Her untimely death marked the end of an era of pioneering exploration and diplomacy in the Middle East.

Gertrude Bell's legacy endures as a testament to the power of exploration, cultural understanding, and diplomacy. Her work in mapping and exploring the Middle East, combined with her significant role in shaping the region's history and politics, solidify her place in history as a trailblazing figure who left an indelible mark on the world.

As we commemorate Gertrude Bell's tireless efforts in mapping and exploring the Middle East and her pivotal role in the region's history, we honor her as a trailblazing explorer and diplomat whose legacy continues to influence the geopolitics of the Middle East.

Chapter 9: Unsung Heroes

Irena Sendler: Rescuing Jewish Children During the Holocaust

In the darkest days of the Holocaust, when humanity was tested beyond imagination, Irena Sendler emerged as a beacon of hope and compassion. Her heroic efforts to rescue Jewish children from the horrors of the Warsaw Ghetto and the Nazi regime's atrocities remain a testament to the indomitable spirit of resistance and humanity's capacity for selflessness in the face of unspeakable evil.

Irena Sendler was born on February 15, 1910, in Warsaw, Poland. From an early age, she demonstrated a deep sense of empathy and a commitment to helping others. Her experiences as a social worker and nurse in Warsaw's impoverished neighborhoods exposed her to the suffering of the most vulnerable members of society.

As World War II engulfed Europe and the Nazis occupied Poland, Irena Sendler's resolve to make a difference became unwavering. In 1940, she joined a network of Polish social workers and activists determined to provide aid and assistance to Jewish families trapped in the Warsaw Ghetto.

One of Sendler's most remarkable contributions was her involvement in the clandestine operation to smuggle Jewish children out of the ghetto. With the support of her colleagues and a forged identity as a nurse, she gained access to the ghetto, risking her life daily to rescue children facing certain death.

Sendler employed various methods to save the lives of Jewish children. She hid them in ambulances, trolleys, and even coffins, often drugging babies to keep them quiet during the dangerous journeys to safety. Once outside the ghetto, she found shelter for the children in convents, orphanages, and with sympathetic Polish families.

Irena Sendler kept meticulous records of the children's real names and their new identities, secretly recording their information on slips of paper and placing them in jars buried beneath an apple tree in her friend's garden. These hidden records, known as the "Jars of Life," would later prove invaluable in reuniting the surviving children with their families.

Tragically, in 1943, Irena Sendler's activities were discovered by the Gestapo, and she was arrested, imprisoned, and subjected to brutal interrogations. Despite enduring torture, she refused to reveal the names or locations of the children she had rescued or her fellow conspirators.

Ultimately, Sendler's arrest spared her life when her colleagues successfully bribed German officials to secure her release. Remarkably, she continued her underground rescue efforts even after her release, assuming a new identity and continuing to assist Jewish families.

The end of World War II brought freedom to Europe, but it also revealed the extent of the Holocaust's horrors. Irena Sendler's bravery and compassion came to light, as survivors began to share their stories of rescue and survival. In 1965, she was recognized by Yad Vashem, the Holocaust memorial in Israel, as one of the "Righteous Among the Nations."

Irena Sendler's heroic actions remained largely unsung for many years, but her story gradually gained recognition. In 2007, she was nominated for the Nobel Peace Prize, a testament to the enduring impact of her courage and humanity.

Irena Sendler passed away on May 12, 2008, but her legacy as a righteous rescuer and unsung hero lives on. Her story continues to inspire generations and serves as a reminder that even in the darkest of times, there are individuals willing to risk everything to save lives and uphold the values of compassion, empathy, and justice.

As we commemorate Irena Sendler's extraordinary courage in rescuing Jewish children during the Holocaust and her unwavering commitment to humanity, we honor her as an unsung hero who illuminated the darkest chapter of history with acts of selflessness and hope.

Hedy Fry: Championing Multiculturalism and Social Justice

Dr. Hedy Fry emerges as a prominent figure whose tireless advocacy and leadership have helped shape Canada's commitment to diversity, inclusivity, and equality. Her dedication to fostering a more inclusive society and addressing issues of social justice exemplifies the transformative power of public service.

Dr. Hedy Fry was born on August 6, 1941, in Trinidad and Tobago, and she later moved to Canada to pursue her education. She earned her medical degree from the University of British Columbia and went on to become a respected physician, specializing in family medicine and psychiatry.

Fry's journey into politics began in the 1990s when she was elected as the Member of Parliament (MP) for Vancouver Centre. Her election marked a historic moment in Canadian politics as she became the first Black female MP in Canada. This milestone was not only a testament to her achievements but also an inspiration for underrepresented communities across the country.

Throughout her political career, Dr. Hedy Fry has been a vocal advocate for multiculturalism and social justice. She has consistently championed policies and initiatives aimed at fostering inclusivity, diversity, and equity. Her leadership has helped advance critical issues related to human rights, immigration, LGBTQ+ rights, and racial equality.

As the Parliamentary Secretary for Multiculturalism, Fry played a pivotal role in promoting Canada's commitment to multiculturalism and intercultural understanding. Her efforts included advocating for policies that celebrate Canada's diverse cultural heritage while ensuring the protection of individual rights and freedoms.

Dr. Fry's commitment to social justice extends beyond her advocacy within Canada. She has been a strong voice on the international stage, addressing global issues such as gender equality, poverty reduction, and access to healthcare. Her work has contributed to Canada's reputation as a leader in promoting human rights and social justice on the world stage.

One of Fry's notable achievements was her role in advancing LGBTQ+ rights in Canada. She was an early supporter of LGBTQ+ rights and played a significant role in pushing for legislative changes that led to the legalization of same-sex marriage in Canada in 2005. Her advocacy for LGBTQ+ rights helped pave the way for greater inclusivity and equality in Canadian society.

Throughout her political career, Hedy Fry has received numerous awards and recognitions for her advocacy and leadership. Her dedication to building a more inclusive and just society continues to inspire individuals and organizations committed to social justice and multiculturalism.

As we commemorate Dr. Hedy Fry's unwavering commitment to multiculturalism, social justice, and human rights, we honor her as a visionary advocate who has helped shape Canada's identity as a diverse and inclusive nation.

Chapter 10: Women in Space and Science Fiction

Valentina Tereshkova: Becoming the First Woman in Space

Valentina Tereshkova shines as a trailblazing figure whose historic journey as the first woman in space not only expanded the boundaries of human exploration but also inspired generations of women to pursue careers in science, technology, engineering, and mathematics (STEM).

Valentina Vladimirovna Tereshkova was born on March 6, 1937, in the village of Maslennikovo, Russia. Her early life was marked by the challenges of World War II and a fascination with aviation, nurtured by her father's interest in flying. Little did she know that her passion for the skies would one day propel her beyond the Earth's atmosphere.

Tereshkova's journey to becoming the first woman in space began in earnest when she joined the Soviet space program in 1961. At the age of 26, she was selected as one of five female cosmonauts for the Vostok 6 mission, a historic flight that would change the course of space exploration.

On June 16, 1963, Valentina Tereshkova made history by embarking on her historic mission aboard the Vostok 6 spacecraft. Her journey into space lasted nearly three days, during which she orbited the Earth 48 times, conducting experiments and collecting data on the effects of space travel on the human body.

Tereshkova's mission was a resounding success and a significant milestone in the Space Race between the United States and the Soviet Union. Her achievement shattered gender barriers and demonstrated that women were just as capable as men in the demanding field of space exploration.

Upon her return to Earth, Valentina Tereshkova became an international symbol of women's achievements in science and technology. She received numerous accolades and honors, including the title of Hero of the Soviet

Union, and she became an ambassador for Soviet and Russian space exploration.

Beyond her historic mission, Tereshkova's legacy extends to her advocacy for STEM education and her role as a prominent political figure in Russia. She served as a member of the Soviet and later Russian parliaments, where she continued to champion the advancement of science and technology.

Valentina Tereshkova's journey into space not only expanded our understanding of human capabilities in the cosmos but also paved the way for future generations of female astronauts and scientists. Her accomplishments serve as a testament to the power of determination and the capacity of women to excel in traditionally male-dominated fields.

As we commemorate Valentina Tereshkova's groundbreaking journey as the first woman in space and her enduring impact on the field of space exploration and STEM education, we honor her as a trailblazing figure who defied gravity and inspired the world to reach for the stars.

Nichelle Nichols: Breaking Racial Barriers on "Star Trek"

In the world of science fiction and cultural representation, Nichelle Nichols stands as a trailblazing figure whose portrayal of Lieutenant Uhura on the iconic television series "Star Trek" not only transcended racial barriers but also inspired a generation of viewers to imagine a future where diversity and inclusion were central to the human experience.

Nichelle Nichols, born on December 28, 1932, in Robbins, Illinois, began her career in entertainment as a singer and actress. Her early accomplishments included performing with renowned artists such as Duke Ellington and Lionel Hampton. However, it was her groundbreaking role as Lieutenant Uhura on "Star Trek" that would cement her place in history.

"Star Trek," created by Gene Roddenberry, made its television debut in 1966 during a tumultuous period in American history marked by civil rights struggles and social upheaval. At a time when racial segregation was still a painful reality in many parts of the United States, Nichols' role as Uhura was groundbreaking.

Nichelle Nichols' portrayal of Lieutenant Uhura was historic for several reasons. She was one of the first Black women to have a prominent and recurring role on a major television series, and her character held a position of authority and responsibility as the communications officer on the starship USS Enterprise.

Perhaps one of the most pivotal moments in Nichelle Nichols' career came when she considered leaving "Star Trek" after the first season. It was none other than Dr. Martin Luther King Jr. himself who urged her to stay on the show. He recognized the cultural significance of her role and its potential to challenge racial stereotypes and inspire African Americans to pursue careers in science and technology.

Nichols' decision to remain on "Star Trek" proved momentous. Her character's interactions with other crew members, including the famous interracial kiss with Captain James T. Kirk (played by William Shatner), broke new ground in television and challenged societal norms of the time.

Beyond her on-screen contributions, Nichelle Nichols' presence at conventions and public events allowed her to interact with fans, many of whom were inspired by her character and her role as a pioneering African American actress. She used her platform to advocate for diversity in the entertainment industry and to encourage young people to pursue careers in STEM fields.

Nichelle Nichols' legacy extends far beyond her time on "Star Trek." Her impact on popular culture and her role in promoting diversity and inclusion in the realm of science fiction continue to resonate with audiences around the world. Her influence can be seen in the diverse cast of subsequent "Star Trek" series and in the broader movement for representation in entertainment.

As we commemorate Nichelle Nichols' groundbreaking portrayal of Lieutenant Uhura on "Star Trek" and her enduring impact on breaking racial barriers in the realm of science fiction and entertainment, we honor her as a trailblazing figure who boldly went where few had gone before, inspiring generations to imagine a future where diversity and equality are fundamental principles.

Mary Shelley: Pioneering Science Fiction with "Frankenstein"

Mary Shelley stands as a visionary figure whose groundbreaking novel "Frankenstein; or, The Modern Prometheus" not only gave birth to the science fiction genre but also explored profound themes of ethics, technology, and the consequences of human ambition.

Mary Wollstonecraft Shelley was born on August 30, 1797, in London, England, into a family of intellectuals and writers. Her mother, Mary Wollstonecraft, was a renowned feminist philosopher, and her father, William Godwin, was a prominent political philosopher and novelist. These intellectual influences played a significant role in shaping her worldview and literary ambitions.

Mary Shelley's life was marked by personal tragedies, including the early death of her mother and the suicide of her half-sister, Fanny Imlay. These experiences, along with her tumultuous relationship with the poet Percy Bysshe Shelley, deeply influenced her writing and provided the emotional backdrop for her most famous work.

In 1816, Mary Shelley and Percy Shelley, along with Lord Byron and John Polidori, embarked on a trip to Lake Geneva, Switzerland. During their stay, they engaged in a competition to write ghost stories. It was during this time that Mary Shelley conceived the idea for "Frankenstein."

Published in 1818, "Frankenstein" tells the story of Victor Frankenstein, a young scientist who, driven by ambition and the desire to conquer death, creates a grotesque and intelligent creature through a series of scientific experiments. The novel explores themes of creation, responsibility, and the consequences of unchecked scientific advancement.

One of the novel's most enduring and compelling aspects is the moral and ethical questions it raises. Mary Shelley's portrayal of Victor Frankenstein's disregard for the ethical implications of his actions and his failure to take responsibility for his creation has made "Frankenstein" a timeless cautionary tale about the consequences of scientific hubris.

"Frankenstein" is often considered the first science fiction novel, as it introduced the concept of using science and technology to explore the boundaries of human knowledge and the potential for both creation and destruction. The novel's enduring popularity and cultural significance have cemented Mary Shelley's place as a pioneer of the science fiction genre.

Mary Shelley's legacy extends beyond "Frankenstein." Her life and work continue to inspire writers, scientists, and thinkers who grapple with the ethical and philosophical implications of technological advancement and the pursuit of knowledge. Her exploration of complex moral dilemmas remains relevant in the modern age of scientific discovery and innovation.

As we commemorate Mary Shelley's pioneering contributions to science fiction and her exploration of profound themes in "Frankenstein," we honor her as a visionary author who ignited the imagination of generations and continues to challenge our understanding of science, ethics, and human nature.

Sally Ride: Inspiring a Generation as an Astronaut

Sally Ride emerges as an iconic figure whose historic journey as the first American woman in space not only shattered gender barriers but also ignited the dreams and aspirations of countless young people, especially girls, to reach for the stars.

Sally Kristen Ride was born on May 26, 1951, in Encino, California. Her early passion for science and athletics set the stage for her remarkable journey into space. Ride earned a bachelor's degree in physics from Stanford University and a Ph.D. in astrophysics, becoming one of the first American women to achieve this distinction.

In 1978, NASA announced its first class of female astronauts, known as the "Thirty-Five New Guys." Sally Ride's selection as an astronaut marked a pivotal moment in the history of space exploration. On June 18, 1983, she made history by becoming the first American woman to travel to space aboard the Space Shuttle Challenger during the STS-7 mission.

Sally Ride's journey into space not only captured the imagination of the nation but also symbolized a significant step toward gender equality in the field of astronautics. Her accomplishments challenged stereotypes and encouraged young women to pursue careers in science, technology, engineering, and mathematics (STEM).

Beyond her pioneering achievement, Sally Ride's contributions to space science were substantial. She conducted experiments related to astrophysics and Earth sciences during her missions and contributed to the understanding of the Earth's atmosphere and the effects of solar radiation.

Sally Ride's impact extended to her role as a science communicator and advocate for STEM education. She co-founded Sally Ride Science, an organization dedicated to inspiring young people, especially girls, to pursue STEM fields. Through her books and speaking engagements, she sought to make science more accessible and engaging for all.

Tragically, Sally Ride passed away on July 23, 2012, but her legacy endures. Her life's work and her passion for space exploration continue to inspire generations of astronauts, scientists, and young people who are drawn to the wonders of the cosmos and the potential for discovery beyond Earth.

As we commemorate Sally Ride's historic journey as the first American woman in space, her dedication to STEM education, and her enduring impact on inspiring future generations, we honor her as a trailblazing astronaut and educator who blazed a trail among the stars and illuminated the path for others to follow.

Chapter 11: Women in Mathematics

Emmy Noether: Revolutionizing Abstract Algebra and Symmetry in Mathematics

In the world of mathematics, where the beauty of abstraction meets the rigor of logic, Emmy Noether stands as an indomitable force who reshaped the very foundations of the discipline. Her pioneering work in abstract algebra and symmetry laid the groundwork for some of the most profound discoveries in mathematics and science, despite facing societal and professional barriers as a woman in academia.

Emmy Noether was born on March 23, 1882, in Erlangen, Germany, into a family deeply rooted in mathematics. Her father, Max Noether, was a renowned mathematician, and Emmy inherited his passion for the subject. She pursued her studies at the University of Erlangen, where she initially faced obstacles due to her gender. In an era when women were often excluded from higher education, Noether's determination and talent prevailed.

As Noether embarked on her academic journey, she encountered the vibrant mathematical community of Göttingen, Germany, which would become her intellectual home. Under the mentorship of the eminent mathematician David Hilbert, she began to make her mark. Her groundbreaking work in the theory of invariants and its application to abstract algebra laid the foundation for what would later become known as Noether's theorem.

Noether's theorem, which she published in 1915, remains one of the most profound and consequential results in physics and mathematics. It established a deep connection between the symmetries of physical systems and the conservation laws that govern them. Simply put, it revealed that for every symmetry in a physical system, there exists a corresponding conservation law.

This theorem, while abstract in nature, had profound implications in the realm of physics. It played a crucial role in the development of Albert Einstein's theory of general relativity and the formulation of quantum mechanics. Noether's work enabled physicists to better understand the fundamental principles that govern the universe.

Despite her groundbreaking contributions, Emmy Noether faced discrimination throughout her career due to her gender. She worked for many years without a formal position and often received meager pay compared to her male colleagues. Nevertheless, her dedication to mathematics remained unwavering.

During her time at Bryn Mawr College in the United States, Noether continued her groundbreaking research and mentored numerous students, both male and female, who went on to become distinguished mathematicians themselves. She influenced a generation of scholars and left an indelible mark on the field of mathematics.

Tragically, Emmy Noether's life was cut short when she died of complications following surgery in 1935. Her contributions, however, live on as a testament to the power of perseverance, intellectual brilliance, and the pursuit of knowledge.

Today, Emmy Noether is celebrated as one of the greatest mathematicians of the 20th century. Her work continues to inspire mathematicians, physicists, and scientists across the globe. The Emmy Noether Society, founded in her honor, promotes the advancement of women in mathematics, ensuring that her legacy endures as a beacon of equality and excellence in the mathematical world.

Emmy Noether's story serves as a powerful reminder that talent knows no gender boundaries, and that even in the face of adversity, the pursuit of knowledge and the quest for truth can lead to groundbreaking discoveries that shape the course of human understanding.

Katherine Johnson: Breaking Racial Barriers at NASA and Calculating Trajectories for Space Missions

In the annals of space exploration, Katherine Johnson stands as a brilliant mathematician whose precise calculations played a pivotal role in propelling humanity into the cosmos. Her remarkable journey at NASA, where she overcame racial and gender barriers, remains a testament to her intellect, resilience, and the indomitable spirit that led her to calculate trajectories for some of the most iconic space missions in history.

Katherine Coleman Goble Johnson was born on August 26, 1918, in White Sulphur Springs, West Virginia. From a young age, her mathematical prowess was evident, and she quickly outpaced her peers in the classroom. Encouraged by her parents, who recognized her exceptional talent, Katherine's educational journey led her to graduate summa cum laude from West Virginia State College with degrees in mathematics and French.

In 1953, Katherine Johnson's journey to NASA began when she joined the all-black West Area Computing section at the National Advisory Committee for Aeronautics (NACA), which later became NASA. Segregation and racial discrimination were pervasive at the time, but her intellect soon transcended the boundaries imposed by prejudice.

Katherine's mathematical expertise led her to perform critical calculations for engineers and scientists. Her role was especially significant during the Space Race, where the United States aimed to surpass the Soviet Union in space exploration. Katherine's calculations were indispensable for trajectory analysis, launch windows, and reentry paths.

One of her most notable contributions was her work on John Glenn's historic orbit of Earth in 1962. Glenn insisted that Katherine personally verify the calculations for his mission, stating that he would not fly unless "the girl" confirmed the numbers. Her meticulous work provided the confidence needed for the mission's success.

Katherine Johnson's brilliance extended beyond the Earth's orbit. She played a pivotal role in calculating the trajectory for the Apollo 11 mission, which landed astronauts Neil Armstrong and Buzz Aldrin on the Moon in 1969. Her calculations ensured the safe return of the astronauts to Earth, a task that required extraordinary precision and expertise.

Throughout her career, Katherine faced challenges as one of the few African American women in the predominantly white, male world of NASA. Her dedication to her work and her unfaltering resolve to excel in her field not only earned her the respect of her colleagues but also paved the way for future generations of women and minority scientists and engineers.

Katherine Johnson's contributions remained relatively unknown to the wider public until the release of the book "Hidden Figures" by Margot Lee Shetterly and the subsequent film adaptation. These works brought Katherine's story to the forefront, celebrating her trailblazing achievements and the critical role she played in America's space exploration efforts.

Katherine Johnson continued to work at NASA until her retirement in 1986. In 2015, she was awarded the Presidential Medal of Freedom for her pioneering contributions to science and mathematics. Her legacy endures as an inspiration to aspiring scientists and as a symbol of the triumph of intellect and determination over adversity.

Katherine Johnson's remarkable journey through the segregated world of science and her invaluable contributions to space exploration serve as a beacon of hope, reminding us all that the boundaries of possibility are limitless when guided by intelligence, perseverance, and a commitment to breaking down barriers.

Maryam Mirzakhani: Becoming the First Woman to Win the Fields Medal for Contributions to Geometry

In the books of pure mathematics, Maryam Mirzakhani's brilliance illuminated the path less traveled, leading her to groundbreaking discoveries in the complex and abstract world of geometry. Her remarkable journey culminated in a historic achievement: becoming the first woman to be awarded the Fields Medal, the most prestigious honor in mathematics, for her profound contributions to the field.

Maryam Mirzakhani was born on May 3, 1977, in Tehran, Iran. From an early age, her fascination with mathematics was apparent, and her exceptional talent earned her recognition and support from her teachers and mentors. Her journey into mathematics began at the Farzanegan School, an institution for gifted students in Tehran.

After completing her undergraduate studies at the Sharif University of Technology in Tehran, Maryam pursued a Ph.D. in mathematics at Harvard University under the guidance of renowned mathematician Curtis McMullen. Her doctoral research delved into the intricate world of hyperbolic geometry and Teichmüller dynamics, subjects that would become central to her future work.

One of Maryam's most significant breakthroughs came in her research on moduli spaces of Riemann surfaces, particularly those with handlebody structures. Her work shed new light on the complex dynamics of these surfaces, paving the way for advancements in a wide range of mathematical fields.

In 2014, Maryam Mirzakhani made history by being awarded the Fields Medal, often described as the "Nobel Prize of Mathematics." Her achievement was not merely a recognition of her extraordinary mathematical talent but also a testament to her perseverance and dedication to pushing the boundaries of knowledge.

Her work went beyond her own groundbreaking research. Maryam actively encouraged and mentored young mathematicians, especially women, promoting diversity and inclusivity in the field. She understood the importance of representation and was a role model for aspiring mathematicians worldwide.

Tragically, Maryam Mirzakhani's life was cut short when she succumbed to breast cancer on July 14, 2017, at the age of 40. Her untimely passing was a profound loss to the mathematical community and to the world.

Maryam Mirzakhani's legacy endures through her pioneering contributions to mathematics and her role as a trailblazer for women in the field. Her Fields Medal was a symbol of her extraordinary intellect and the recognition of her dedication to expanding our understanding of the mathematical universe.

Her story serves as a source of inspiration for future generations of mathematicians, especially young women, who aspire to follow in her footsteps. Maryam Mirzakhani's name is etched in history not only as the first woman to win the Fields Medal but also as a luminary whose brilliance continues to illuminate the world of mathematics, reminding us of the limitless possibilities that await those who dare to explore the beauty and intricacy of the mathematical realm.

Chapter 12: Visionary Women in Education

Maria Montessori: Transforming Education Through the Montessori Method

In the field of education, Maria Montessori's name stands as a beacon of innovation and progress. Her groundbreaking work in child development and the creation of the Montessori method revolutionized the way children are educated, emphasizing independence, self-directed learning, and the nurturing of a child's natural curiosity.

Maria Tecla Artemisia Montessori was born on August 31, 1870, in Chiaravalle, Italy. Her journey into education began with a background in medicine. She was one of the first Italian women to attend medical school, where she specialized in psychiatry and pedagogy.

It was during her work with intellectually disabled children at the Orthophrenic School in Rome that Maria Montessori began to formulate her innovative ideas about education. She believed that every child had the potential to learn and thrive, regardless of their background or abilities.

In 1907, Montessori opened her first Casa dei Bambini, or "Children's House," in a working-class district of Rome. This marked the birth of the Montessori method, a child-centered approach to education that emphasized self-discovery and hands-on learning. Her classroom was carefully designed with child-sized furniture and materials that encouraged exploration and independence.

One of the key principles of the Montessori method is the belief that children are naturally curious and should be allowed to follow their interests at their own pace. Montessori teachers serve as guides rather than traditional instructors, fostering an environment where children take the lead in their learning journey.

Another hallmark of the Montessori method is the use of self-correcting materials, which allow children to identify and learn from their mistakes independently. This approach empowers children to develop problem-solving skills and a sense of autonomy in their learning process.

Maria Montessori's innovative approach to education quickly gained recognition and acclaim. Her method spread across Europe and later to the United States, where it continues to thrive in Montessori schools and classrooms around the world.

Montessori's impact extended beyond her classrooms. She wrote extensively on her educational philosophy and published several books, including "The Montessori Method" and "The Secret of Childhood." Her writings further popularized her approach and inspired educators and parents to adopt Montessori principles.

Throughout her life, Maria Montessori remained dedicated to the welfare and education of children. She conducted extensive research on child development, and her work contributed significantly to our understanding of how children learn and grow.

Maria Montessori passed away on May 6, 1952, but her legacy endures through the countless children who have benefited from her educational philosophy. Montessori schools continue to flourish, offering children an environment where they can develop into independent, self-motivated learners.

Maria Montessori's vision of education, grounded in respect for the child's innate abilities and potential, continues to shape the way we educate and nurture future generations. Her legacy serves as a reminder that the most profound changes in society often begin with innovative and compassionate approaches to education, and that every child has the capacity to become a self-directed learner and a contributor to a better world.

Malala Yousafzai: Advocating for Girls' Education and Becoming the Youngest Nobel Laureate

In the heart of Pakistan's Swat Valley, a young girl's unwavering determination and courage would come to symbolize the global fight for girls' education. Malala Yousafzai's remarkable journey from a courageous student to an advocate for girls' rights and the youngest Nobel laureate serves as an inspirational tale of resilience, activism, and the belief that education can change the world.

Malala was born on July 12, 1997, in Mingora, Swat Valley, Pakistan, into a family that valued education. Her father, Ziauddin Yousafzai, was an educator and an activist, and he instilled in Malala a deep appreciation for learning and the importance of speaking out against injustice.

The Swat Valley, once known for its breathtaking beauty, became a battleground for the Taliban's oppressive regime, which sought to restrict girls' access to education. In this hostile environment, Malala's courage shone brightly. At a young age, she began writing a blog for BBC Urdu under a pseudonym, where she candidly shared her experiences and her fervent desire for education.

Malala's advocacy for girls' education did not go unnoticed. Her increasing visibility made her a target of the Taliban, who attempted to assassinate her on her way to school in October 2012. Malala survived the attack, but it left her with life-threatening injuries. Her resilience in the face of adversity, along with global outrage and support, propelled her to the forefront of the fight for girls' education.

Following her recovery, Malala and her family settled in Birmingham, England. There, she continued her education and advocacy work with even greater determination. Her foundation, the Malala Fund, was established to advocate for girls' right to twelve years of free, safe, and quality education.

Malala's unwavering commitment to her cause earned her international acclaim. In 2013, she delivered a powerful speech at the United Nations, calling for universal access to education and declaring that "one child, one teacher, one book, and one pen can change the world." Her impassioned plea resonated with people worldwide.

In 2014, Malala became the youngest recipient of the Nobel Peace Prize, at the age of 17. Her dedication to education and her fearless advocacy had not only inspired a generation but also ignited a global movement to ensure that girls everywhere have the opportunity to learn.

Malala's impact extends far beyond her accolades. She continues to travel the world, meeting with world leaders, advocating for policy changes, and championing the cause of education. Her memoir, "I Am Malala," has become a bestseller, spreading her message of hope and empowerment.

Malala's story serves as a beacon of hope for girls worldwide who face barriers to education. Her courage in the face of adversity reminds us that the pursuit of knowledge is a fundamental right, and it is worth standing up for, no matter the challenges.

Today, Malala Yousafzai is a symbol of courage, resilience, and the transformative power of education. Her advocacy has catalyzed change, bringing us one step closer to a world where every girl can access quality education and fulfill her potential. In Malala's words, "Let us make our future now, and let us make our dreams tomorrow's reality."

Anna Julia Cooper: Promoting Education and Civil Rights for African American Women

In the turbulent years following the American Civil War, Anna Julia Cooper emerged as a pioneering scholar, educator, and advocate for the rights of African American women. Her unwavering commitment to education, civil rights, and gender equality left an indelible mark on history and laid the groundwork for the civil rights and women's rights movements of the 20th century.

Anna Julia Haywood was born on August 10, 1858, in Raleigh, North Carolina, during the era of slavery. Her early life was marked by adversity and challenges, but she demonstrated a thirst for knowledge from a young age. At the age of 9, she was enrolled in St. Augustine's Normal School and Collegiate Institute, a school founded by the Episcopal Church to educate newly freed African Americans.

Anna's dedication to education was evident throughout her life. She pursued higher education at Oberlin College in Ohio, where she became one of the first African American women to earn a bachelor's degree in 1884. She later earned a master's degree in mathematics from the same institution, a remarkable achievement given the prevailing racial and gender biases of the time.

Anna's journey as an educator and activist took her to Washington, D.C., where she became the principal of the Preparatory High School for Colored Youth, now known as Dunbar High School. Under her leadership, the school flourished, and Anna advocated for a curriculum that emphasized both academic excellence and character development.

It was during this period that Anna Julia Cooper began to publish her seminal work, "A Voice from the South by a Black Woman of the South," which was a pioneering piece of literature at the intersection of race and gender. In this book, she eloquently argued for the education and empowerment of African American women, stressing that their progress was essential for the advancement of the entire community.

Anna's advocacy extended to civil rights and suffrage. She was an active member of various organizations and associations, including the Colored Women's League and the NAACP. Her commitment to women's rights was reflected in her participation in the International Council of Women and the National American Woman Suffrage Association.

Throughout her life, Anna Julia Cooper championed the rights and voices of African American women. She argued that education and empowerment were the keys to overcoming oppression and inequality. Her legacy continues to inspire generations of activists and scholars who strive for justice and equality.

Anna Julia Cooper's impact on education, civil rights, and women's rights remains profound. Her vision of empowerment through education, her commitment to racial and gender equality, and her fearless advocacy for justice have left an enduring legacy. She stands as a testament to the enduring power of education and the indomitable spirit of those who dedicate their lives to the pursuit of equality and justice for all.

Dorothy Vaughan: Pioneering Computing at NASA and Mentoring a Generation of African American Mathematicians

In the midst of the space race and the struggle for civil rights in America, Dorothy Vaughan emerged as a trailblazing mathematician and computer scientist whose contributions to NASA's early space missions were pivotal. Her remarkable career, marked by innovation and mentorship, not only advanced space exploration but also opened doors for African American women in the field of mathematics and engineering.

Dorothy Johnson Vaughan was born on September 20, 1910, in Kansas City, Missouri. From an early age, she exhibited a keen aptitude for mathematics and an insatiable curiosity about the world around her. After graduating from Wilberforce University in Ohio, she began her teaching career, but her passion for mathematics eventually led her to a different path.

In 1943, Dorothy Vaughan joined the National Advisory Committee for Aeronautics (NACA), which would later become NASA, as a "computer." In this era, the term "computer" referred not to machines but to the individuals, primarily women, who performed complex mathematical calculations by hand. Vaughan's exceptional skills and her ability to tackle complex calculations made her an invaluable asset to NACA.

As the demands of aeronautical research grew, NACA transitioned to using electronic computers. Recognizing the significance of this technological shift, Dorothy Vaughan took the initiative to learn the FORTRAN programming language, making her one of the first African American employees at NACA to become proficient in computer programming. Her expertise in programming the early IBM computers was instrumental in ensuring the success of critical projects.

One of the most notable achievements in Vaughan's career was her role in the launch of the first American astronaut, Alan Shepard, into space in 1961. She and her team were responsible for calculating the trajectories and flight paths for the Mercury-Redstone 3 mission, which sent Shepard into space for a historic 15-minute suborbital flight.

Beyond her groundbreaking work, Dorothy Vaughan played a pivotal role in mentoring and advocating for African American women in mathematics and engineering. She recognized the barriers they faced in a predominantly white, male field and worked tirelessly to create opportunities for them. Vaughan was a founding member of the National Technical Association, an organization dedicated to promoting the professional development of African Americans in engineering and science.

Dorothy Vaughan's legacy is also celebrated through the portrayal of her character in the book "Hidden Figures" by Margot Lee Shetterly and the subsequent film adaptation. The book and movie shed light on the significant contributions of Vaughan and other African American women at NASA during the early days of the space program.

Dorothy Vaughan retired from NASA in 1971, leaving behind a legacy of trailblazing achievements and unwavering commitment to equality and mentorship. Her pioneering work in computing and her dedication to breaking racial and gender barriers continue to inspire generations of mathematicians, engineers, and scientists.

Dorothy Vaughan's journey serves as a reminder that progress in science and technology is often driven by the determination and innovation of individuals like her, who use their talents to break down barriers and open doors for future generations. Her contributions to space exploration and her advocacy for diversity and inclusion continue to shape the fields of mathematics and engineering today.

Chapter 13: Women in Environmental Conservation

Wangari Maathai: Initiating the Green Belt Movement in Kenya and Planting Millions of Trees

In the heart of Kenya's lush landscapes, a visionary woman named Wangari Maathai embarked on a mission that would not only transform the environment but also empower communities and inspire a global movement. Her founding of the Green Belt Movement, accompanied by her tireless efforts to plant millions of trees, stands as a testament to the power of grassroots activism and the ability of one person to effect positive change.

Wangari Maathai was born on April 1, 1940, in Nyeri, Kenya. From an early age, she displayed a passion for learning and the natural world, which would become driving forces in her life. After completing her education in Kenya and the United States, including earning a Ph.D. in biology from the University of Nairobi, Wangari returned to her homeland with a deep sense of purpose.

In the 1970s, Kenya, like many other countries, faced severe environmental degradation, deforestation, and loss of biodiversity. Wangari witnessed the devastating effects of land degradation on rural communities, particularly women who relied on natural resources for their livelihoods. It was in response to these challenges that she founded the Green Belt Movement in 1977.

The Green Belt Movement's mission was simple yet profoundly impactful: to empower women, improve the environment, and promote sustainable development through tree planting. Wangari recognized that tree planting could combat soil erosion, replenish forests, and provide communities with valuable resources like firewood, timber, and clean water.

Under Wangari's leadership, the Green Belt Movement mobilized thousands of women, often from marginalized rural communities, to become environmental stewards. They were not only taught how to plant trees but also educated about the importance of protecting the environment and advocating for their rights.

One of the Movement's key initiatives was the planting of millions of trees, a task that required community involvement and dedication. Tree-planting ceremonies became powerful symbols of hope, renewal, and empowerment. The trees planted by the Green Belt Movement not only rejuvenated Kenya's landscapes but also served as a source of income and sustenance for the communities involved.

Wangari Maathai's environmental activism was not without its challenges. She faced opposition from those who sought to exploit natural resources for short-term gain, and her advocacy for sustainable development sometimes put her at odds with the government. Despite these obstacles, she remained steadfast in her commitment to both environmental and human rights.

Wangari's work extended beyond Kenya's borders as she became a global advocate for environmental conservation and women's empowerment. In 2004, she was awarded the Nobel Peace Prize for her exceptional contribution to sustainable development, democracy, and peace. She was the first African woman and the first environmentalist to receive this prestigious honor.

Wangari Maathai's legacy lives on through the Green Belt Movement, which continues its work in Kenya and around the world. Her story serves as an inspiration to environmental activists, women's rights advocates, and anyone striving to make a positive impact on the planet.

Wangari's life demonstrates that individual action, fueled by passion and commitment, can catalyze change on a grand scale. Her vision of a greener, more equitable world continues to motivate countless individuals and communities to plant trees, protect the environment, and stand up for their rights.

Greta Thunberg: Inspiring a Global Youth Movement for Climate Action

In the age of social media and digital activism, a young Swedish girl's solo climate strike outside the Swedish parliament ignited a global movement that captured the world's attention. Greta Thunberg, with her unwavering determination and impassioned speeches, has become the face of a youth-led climate movement, demanding urgent action to address the climate crisis and inspiring millions around the world to join her cause.

Greta Thunberg was born on January 3, 2003, in Stockholm, Sweden. From a young age, she displayed a deep concern for environmental issues, particularly climate change. At the age of 15, she decided to take a radical step to draw attention to the climate crisis: she began skipping school every Friday to sit outside the Swedish parliament with a sign that read "Skolstrejk för klimatet" or "School Strike for Climate."

Greta's solo protest, which she called "Fridays for Future," quickly gained traction on social media and attracted the support of fellow students and activists. Her message was simple yet powerful: politicians and leaders were failing to take sufficient action to address the existential threat of climate change, and she demanded immediate and meaningful action.

Greta's speeches and messages were characterized by their stark honesty and unfiltered anger. She condemned the world's leaders for their inaction and accused them of stealing her generation's future. Her passion and authenticity resonated with people of all ages, and she became a symbol of youth activism and hope.

One of the most iconic moments of Greta's activism was her speech at the United Nations Climate Action Summit in 2019. In her impassioned address, she admonished world leaders for their empty promises and lack of concrete action on climate change. Her words, delivered with a mixture of anger and sorrow, reverberated around the world and catapulted her into the international spotlight.

Greta's impact extended beyond her solo strikes and speeches. She inspired millions of students and activists worldwide to join the Fridays for Future movement. Climate strikes, protests, and marches took place in cities across the globe, with students demanding climate action and holding their leaders accountable.

Despite facing criticism and even harassment from some quarters, Greta Thunberg remained steadfast in her mission. She continued to speak truth to power, meet with world leaders, and advocate for climate action on a global scale. Her uncompromising stance and her ability to mobilize young people created a new sense of urgency in the climate movement.

Greta's efforts have earned her numerous accolades and recognitions, including being named Time magazine's Person of the Year in 2019. However, she has consistently redirected the focus to the climate crisis itself, emphasizing that the urgency of the issue far outweighs any individual recognition.

Greta Thunberg's journey is a testament to the power of youth activism and the impact of grassroots movements. Her ability to galvanize a global youth climate strike, engage with world leaders, and inspire millions underscores the potential of individuals, particularly young people, to effect change.

As the world grapples with the climate crisis, Greta Thunberg serves as a symbol of hope and a reminder that collective action is essential. Her call for climate justice, immediate action, and a sustainable future continues to reverberate globally, and she remains an inspirational force for generations to come.

Chapter 14: Female Innovators in Business and Technology

Estée Lauder: Building a Cosmetics Empire and Revolutionizing the Beauty Industry

In the world of beauty and cosmetics, Estée Lauder's name is synonymous with elegance, innovation, and entrepreneurial success. With an unwavering passion for skincare and makeup, she built a cosmetics empire that not only transformed the beauty industry but also paved the way for women entrepreneurs in business and technology.

Estée Lauder, born Josephine Esther Mentzer on July 1, 1906, in Queens, New York, had an early fascination with beauty and skincare, inspired by her Hungarian immigrant mother's homemade face creams. This early exposure sparked her interest in cosmetics and laid the foundation for her future career.

In the 1940s, Estée Lauder and her husband, Joseph Lauder, started their cosmetics company with a few skincare products and a relentless belief in the power of word-of-mouth marketing. They began by selling their products to family and friends and soon expanded to high-end department stores, where Estée personally demonstrated her products and developed a loyal customer base.

One of Estée's early innovations was the introduction of free samples with purchases, a marketing tactic that not only introduced customers to her products but also fostered a sense of luxury and exclusivity. This strategy became a hallmark of the Estée Lauder brand.

Estée's commitment to quality and innovation led to the development of groundbreaking skincare and beauty products. In 1953, the company launched "Youth-Dew," a bath oil that doubled as a perfume, and it became a sensation. It was the first of many iconic products that would define the brand's reputation for luxury and excellence.

Throughout her career, Estée Lauder was a pioneer in promoting the idea that skincare and makeup were essential for women's self-esteem and confidence. Her brand embraced the concept of a daily skincare regimen, which was revolutionary at the time. She also believed in the power of personalized beauty advice and created a unique shopping experience for her customers.

Estée Lauder's innovative approach extended to her use of technology and marketing. She was an early adopter of television advertising, and her commercials featuring her products and her own charismatic presence became legendary. Her keen understanding of the importance of branding and image helped her build a global beauty empire.

One of Estée Lauder's enduring legacies is her commitment to philanthropy. She supported numerous charitable causes, including breast cancer research and education. The Estée Lauder Companies continue this tradition of giving back through the Breast Cancer Campaign and other philanthropic initiatives.

Estée Lauder passed away in 2004, leaving behind a cosmetics empire that has grown to include multiple brands and a global presence. Her dedication to innovation, quality, and the empowerment of women in the beauty industry continues to shape the company's values and mission.

Estée Lauder's journey serves as an inspiration to women in business and technology. She broke down barriers in the male-dominated world of entrepreneurship and proved that determination, innovation, and a passion for one's craft can lead to extraordinary success. Her contributions to the beauty industry and her entrepreneurial spirit have left an indelible mark, and her name remains synonymous with timeless elegance and beauty.

Oprah Winfrey: Building a Media and Entertainment Empire and Becoming a Cultural Icon

In the world of media and entertainment, Oprah Winfrey's name stands as a symbol of empowerment, inspiration, and the limitless possibilities of the American Dream. Her journey from a challenging childhood to becoming a global media mogul, philanthropist, and cultural icon is a testament to her resilience, vision, and the impact of her work.

Oprah Gail Winfrey was born on January 29, 1954, in Kosciusko, Mississippi. Raised in poverty and facing numerous challenges during her early years, including poverty and abuse, Oprah found solace in reading and public speaking. Her exceptional oratory skills were evident from a young age, and she won a full scholarship to Tennessee State University, where she studied communications.

Oprah's career in media began in radio and local television, where she honed her skills as a news anchor and reporter. Her breakthrough came when she hosted a local talk show in Chicago called "AM Chicago," which quickly became the highest-rated talk show in the city. This success led to the nationally syndicated "The Oprah Winfrey Show" in 1986.

Over the course of 25 years, "The Oprah Winfrey Show" became a cultural phenomenon, reaching millions of viewers worldwide. Oprah's empathetic and genuine interviewing style, combined with her ability to connect with people from all walks of life, made her show a platform for inspirational stories, thought-provoking discussions, and a wide range of social and personal issues.

One of the show's defining features was Oprah's commitment to promoting literature and reading. Her Book Club, which recommended and discussed books, played a significant role in encouraging a culture of reading and led to the success of many authors and their works.

Oprah's impact extended beyond television. She ventured into film, co-producing critically acclaimed movies like "The Color Purple" and "Beloved." She also launched her own multimedia company, Harpo Productions, which expanded into publishing, radio, and digital media.

In addition to her remarkable career in media and entertainment, Oprah has used her platform and wealth for philanthropic endeavors. She established the Oprah Winfrey Leadership Academy for Girls in South Africa, providing educational opportunities to young girls facing adversity. Her philanthropic efforts have supported various causes, including education, healthcare, and advocacy for women and children.

Oprah's influence and cultural significance have earned her numerous accolades and distinctions. She has received multiple Daytime Emmy Awards, a Peabody Award, and the Presidential Medal of Freedom. Her impact on popular culture is immeasurable, and she remains a powerful advocate for issues like literacy, equality, and wellness.

As an African American woman who broke through barriers in the media industry, Oprah Winfrey's journey is a source of inspiration for many. Her story demonstrates the transformative power of education, determination, and the ability to connect with others on a deep and meaningful level.

Oprah Winfrey's legacy is not only her media empire but also her commitment to uplifting individuals and communities. Her ability to inspire, motivate, and effect positive change in the world has left an indelible mark on society. Her life's work continues to be a beacon of hope and a reminder that every individual has the potential to achieve greatness and make a difference in the lives of others.

Chapter 15: Women in the Fight for Social Justice

Sojourner Truth: Advocating for Abolition and Women's Rights through Her Powerful "Ain't I a Woman?" Speech

In the tumultuous era of American history marked by slavery and the struggle for women's rights, Sojourner Truth emerged as a powerful and eloquent advocate for both causes. Her famous "Ain't I a Woman?" speech, delivered in 1851, remains a seminal moment in the fight against slavery and gender inequality, exemplifying her unwavering commitment to justice and equality.

Sojourner Truth was born into slavery around 1797 in Swartekill, New York, with the name Isabella Baumfree. She endured the hardships of slavery, including separation from her family, before escaping to freedom in 1826 with her infant daughter. Following her escape, she became an outspoken abolitionist and champion for women's rights.

What set Sojourner Truth apart was her remarkable ability to captivate audiences with her speaking prowess. Standing nearly six feet tall, with a commanding presence and a deep, resonant voice, she left an indelible impression on those who heard her speak. Her experiences as a former slave lent authenticity and urgency to her message.

In 1851, at the Women's Rights Convention in Akron, Ohio, Sojourner Truth delivered her iconic "Ain't I a Woman?" speech. In her address, she forcefully challenged prevailing notions of gender and race, highlighting the hypocrisy of a society that denied the rights and humanity of both enslaved people and women. Her speech drew attention to the intersectionality of oppression, a concept that would gain prominence in later years.

The essence of Sojourner Truth's speech lay in its simplicity and clarity. She asked, "Ain't I a woman?" to emphasize the common humanity of women, regardless of race. She pointed out the physical strength she possessed as a former slave, dispelling the stereotype that women were delicate and weak. Her words resonated deeply with those in attendance, leaving a profound impact on the suffrage and abolition movements.

Sojourner Truth's advocacy extended beyond her speeches. She actively worked with prominent abolitionists and feminists of her time, including Frederick Douglass and Susan B. Anthony. She met with President Abraham Lincoln during the Civil War to discuss issues related to enslaved people and black soldiers.

In 1864, Sojourner Truth dictated her memoir, "The Narrative of Sojourner Truth," which documented her life as an enslaved person and her journey to freedom. Her memoir provided valuable firsthand insights into the brutality of slavery and served as a powerful tool for the abolitionist cause.

Sojourner Truth's tireless efforts helped pave the way for significant social change. The Emancipation Proclamation in 1863 and the eventual passage of the 19th Amendment granting women the right to vote in 1920 were milestones in the fight for justice and equality that she contributed to, even if she did not live to see them realized.

Sojourner Truth's legacy endures as a symbol of resilience, intersectional advocacy, and the power of speaking truth to power. Her "Ain't I a Woman?" speech remains an iconic moment in the struggle for civil rights and gender equality, and her life serves as a testament to the enduring spirit of those who fight for justice and equality in the face of adversity.

Susan B. Anthony: Championing Women's Suffrage and Equal Rights

In the annals of women's history and the fight for equal rights, Susan B. Anthony's name stands as a symbol of unwavering dedication and relentless advocacy. Her tireless efforts in the suffrage movement, which spanned several decades, played a pivotal role in securing the right to vote for women in the United States and laid the groundwork for the broader pursuit of gender equality.

Susan Brownell Anthony was born on February 15, 1820, in Adams, Massachusetts, into a Quaker family with a strong commitment to social justice and equality. From an early age, she was immersed in the values of anti-slavery activism and women's rights, which would come to define her life's work.

One of Susan B. Anthony's earliest experiences with gender inequality occurred when she became a teacher. She discovered that male teachers earned significantly higher salaries than their female counterparts, sparking her determination to rectify this injustice. However, her path to activism truly took flight when she met fellow activist Elizabeth Cady Stanton in 1851.

Susan B. Anthony and Elizabeth Cady Stanton formed a formidable partnership in the suffrage movement. Together, they dedicated themselves to advancing women's rights and achieving the right to vote. Anthony was known for her organizing skills and tireless commitment to the cause, while Stanton's eloquent speeches and writings added intellectual depth to their efforts.

One of Susan B. Anthony's most significant contributions to the suffrage movement was her tireless advocacy for a women's right to vote. She believed that suffrage was the key to addressing other inequalities that women faced. Anthony and Stanton founded the National Woman Suffrage Association (NWSA) in 1869, which focused on securing a constitutional amendment granting women the right to vote.

Throughout her life, Susan B. Anthony traveled the country, delivering speeches, organizing conventions, and tirelessly petitioning lawmakers for women's suffrage. Her dedication to the cause earned her the moniker "The Napoleon of the Suffrage Movement." She played a pivotal role in the suffrage referendums in Western states, where women's voting rights were first recognized.

In 1872, Susan B. Anthony famously cast a vote in the presidential election, openly defying the law. She was arrested and subsequently put on trial, where she argued that the Fourteenth Amendment, which granted equal protection under the law, implied that women were citizens with the right to vote. Despite her impassioned defense, she was found guilty and fined, but her actions drew national attention to the suffrage cause.

Susan B. Anthony's advocacy continued until her later years, but she did not live to see the passage of the Nineteenth Amendment in 1920, which granted women the right to vote. She passed away on March 13, 1906, in Rochester, New York.

The legacy of Susan B. Anthony is profound. Her unwavering commitment to women's suffrage and equal rights laid the groundwork for subsequent generations of feminists and activists. Her words, her actions, and her enduring belief in the power of women to effect social change continue to inspire those who work towards a more equitable and just society. Susan B. Anthony's name is forever associated with the tireless struggle for gender equality and the transformative power of persistence and determination.

Ida B. Wells: Fiercely Opposing Lynching and Fighting for African American Civil Rights

In the turbulent and racially divided landscape of late 19th and early 20th century America, Ida B. Wells emerged as a fearless journalist, anti-lynching crusader, and civil rights activist. Her unwavering commitment to justice, equality, and the fight against racial violence left an indelible mark on the struggle for African American civil rights and set a precedent for investigative journalism and activism.

Ida Bell Wells was born into slavery on July 16, 1862, in Holly Springs, Mississippi, just as the Civil War ended. Her parents instilled in her a strong sense of education and self-reliance, and she grew up in the tumultuous years of Reconstruction when African Americans began to assert their rights as free citizens.

Wells's life took a drastic turn when her parents and brother died in a yellow fever epidemic in 1878, leaving her responsible for raising her siblings. She found work as a teacher and eventually moved to Memphis, Tennessee, where she continued her teaching career.

In Memphis, Wells's life took another significant turn when she became a journalist. She wrote articles for the "Living Way" newspaper, and her investigative reporting led her to expose the brutal realities of lynching in the

South. After the lynching of three of her friends in 1892, she penned a scathing editorial condemning the practice. This act of journalistic courage and defiance marked the beginning of her anti-lynching crusade.

Ida B. Wells's investigative work and advocacy brought international attention to the horrors of lynching, dispelling the myth that it was a response to black criminality and revealing it as a tool of white supremacy and terrorism. She embarked on speaking tours in the United States and Europe, urging governments and organizations to take action against lynching and racial violence.

Wells's activism extended to her leadership roles in civil rights organizations. She helped found the National Association of Colored Women (NACW) and was a co-founder of the National Association for the Advancement of Colored People (NAACP). Her work in these organizations focused on addressing a wide range of racial injustices beyond lynching, including voter suppression and discrimination.

Throughout her life, Ida B. Wells faced significant personal risks and threats to her safety due to her advocacy. Her printing press in Memphis was destroyed by a mob, and she was forced to relocate to the North for her safety. Nevertheless, she persisted in her fight for justice and equality.

In addition to her activism, Wells was a prolific writer. Her works include "Southern Horrors: Lynch Law in All Its Phases" and "The Red Record," both of which meticulously documented cases of lynching and their underlying causes. Her writings provided an irrefutable record of the horrors of lynching and served as a catalyst for change.

Ida B. Wells passed away on March 25, 1931, in Chicago, Illinois, but her legacy endures as an inspiration to journalists, activists, and advocates for civil rights. Her unyielding commitment to exposing and combating racial violence and injustice, her fearless journalism, and her leadership in civil rights organizations contributed significantly to the broader struggle for racial equality in the United States. Ida B. Wells's name stands as a symbol of courage and a reminder that individuals can effect profound change when they dedicate themselves to the pursuit of justice and equality.

Dolores Huerta: Co-founding the United Farm Workers and Advocating for Farmworker Rights

In the heart of the American agricultural landscape, amidst the struggles of farmworkers and laborers, Dolores Huerta emerged as a pioneering activist and organizer who dedicated her life to improving the working conditions and rights of some of the nation's most vulnerable workers. Her co-founding of the United Farm Workers (UFW) and relentless advocacy reshaped the labor movement and advanced the cause of farmworker rights.

Dolores Clara Fernández was born on April 10, 1930, in Dawson, New Mexico. Her early experiences living and working in farming communities exposed her to the hardships and injustices endured by farmworkers, many of whom were of Mexican and Filipino descent. These experiences ignited her passion for social justice and activism.

Huerta's journey as a labor organizer began in the 1950s when she joined the Community Service Organization (CSO), a grassroots group focused on improving the lives of Hispanic communities. It was here that she honed her organizing skills and became a tireless advocate for workers' rights.

In 1962, Dolores Huerta co-founded the National Farm Workers Association (NFWA), later known as the United Farm Workers (UFW), with Cesar Chavez. Together, they embarked on a mission to address the deplorable working conditions, low wages, and lack of labor protections faced by farmworkers. Huerta's role in the organization was instrumental in building a powerful grassroots movement.

One of the most iconic moments in Dolores Huerta's activism came in 1965 when the UFW launched the Delano grape strike, a protest against unfair labor practices in California's grape fields. Huerta played a pivotal role in organizing the strike, mobilizing farmworkers, and garnering public support. The strike lasted for five years and led to the first labor contracts for farmworkers in the United States, improving wages and working conditions.

Huerta's leadership extended to nonviolent protests and acts of civil disobedience. She was a driving force behind the UFW's boycotts of table grapes and lettuce, which galvanized consumers across the nation to support the farmworkers' cause. Her rallying cry, "Sí, se puede" (Yes, we can), became a powerful slogan for the labor movement.

Dolores Huerta's advocacy extended beyond labor issues. She championed women's rights, advocating for gender equality within the labor movement and society at large. Her commitment to intersectionality and inclusivity made her a trailblazer for both labor and feminist movements.

Throughout her career, Huerta faced numerous challenges, including threats, violence, and arrests. She persisted in the face of adversity, always standing up for the rights of the marginalized and the oppressed.

Dolores Huerta's activism and leadership have been recognized with numerous awards and honors, including the Presidential Medal of Freedom in 2012. Her legacy continues to inspire generations of activists and advocates for social justice. At the age of 91, she remains an active voice for farmworker rights and social change.

Dolores Huerta's life and work remind us of the power of grassroots organizing, the importance of standing up for the rights of the most vulnerable members of society, and the enduring impact of individuals who dedicate themselves to the pursuit of justice. Her legacy stands as a testament to the profound change that can be achieved through tenacity, compassion, and unwavering commitment to the betterment of others.

Chapter 16: Women in the World of Sports

Wilma Rudolph: Overcoming Childhood Illness to Become an Olympic Sprinter and Three-Time Gold Medalist

In the world of sports, where speed and strength reign supreme, Wilma Rudolph's journey from a childhood marked by illness and adversity to becoming an Olympic sprinting sensation is nothing short of remarkable. Her indomitable spirit, determination, and athletic prowess not only earned her three gold medals but also inspired generations of athletes and women to overcome obstacles and achieve greatness.

Wilma Glodean Rudolph was born on June 23, 1940, in St. Bethlehem, Tennessee, the 20th of 22 siblings. Her early years were characterized by poverty and illness. She contracted polio at the age of four, a debilitating disease that left her with weakened legs and necessitated the use of leg braces.

Despite the grim prognosis, Wilma Rudolph's mother, Blanche, refused to accept her daughter's limited mobility as her fate. She embarked on a relentless journey of physical therapy and treatment, often massaging Wilma's legs for hours each day. Wilma's own determination and the unwavering support of her family became the bedrock upon which her future success was built.

Remarkably, by the age of 12, Wilma Rudolph had shed her leg braces and was able to walk unaided. Her incredible recovery fueled her passion for sports, particularly track and field. She joined the basketball and track teams in high school and quickly showcased her remarkable speed and talent as a sprinter.

At the 1960 Rome Olympics, Wilma Rudolph etched her name into the annals of sports history. She competed in the 100 meters, 200 meters, and 4x100 meters relay events. In a display of unparalleled speed and determination, she not only won three gold medals but also set world records in all three events. Her triumph was particularly poignant as she became the first American woman to accomplish such a feat.

Wilma Rudolph's success at the Olympics catapulted her to international stardom and made her an inspiration to countless individuals, especially those facing physical challenges. She was celebrated not only for her athletic achievements but also for her grace, humility, and commitment to civil rights causes.

In the wake of her Olympic success, Rudolph continued to be a trailblazer. She retired from competitive athletics but remained involved in sports by coaching and mentoring young athletes. She also used her platform to advocate for civil rights and racial equality during a tumultuous era in the United States.

Wilma Rudolph's life and legacy remind us that greatness can emerge from adversity. Her story is a testament to the power of perseverance, the importance of familial support, and the boundless potential within each individual. She shattered records, broke barriers, and left an indelible mark on the world of sports, all while embodying the spirit of resilience and triumph over adversity. Wilma Rudolph's legacy continues to inspire athletes and individuals alike to strive for greatness and to overcome the odds, no matter the obstacles they face.

Billie Jean King: Championing Gender Equality in Sports and Defeating Bobby Riggs in the "Battle of the Sexes"

Billie Jean King stands as a trailblazer who reshaped the landscape of women's tennis and championed equal opportunities for female athletes. Her legendary victory in the "Battle of the Sexes" against Bobby Riggs became a defining moment in the fight for gender equity in sports and beyond.

Billie Jean Moffitt was born on November 22, 1943, in Long Beach, California. From an early age, she displayed exceptional talent and determination in tennis. Her remarkable journey to the pinnacle of the sport began in earnest when she won her first Wimbledon title in 1961 at the age of 17.

Throughout the 1960s and 1970s, Billie Jean King dominated women's tennis, amassing a stunning collection of titles and championships. Her tenacity, agility, and strategic prowess on the court made her a formidable force. Yet, as she achieved success in her sport, she also became acutely aware of the glaring disparities in prize money, recognition, and opportunities between male and female athletes.

In 1973, Billie Jean King took a courageous and historic step by founding the Women's Tennis Association (WTA), an organization dedicated to promoting women's tennis and advocating for gender equality within the sport. Her commitment to leveling the playing field extended beyond tennis courts, as she became a vocal proponent for equal pay for female athletes and equal access to sports facilities.

One of the most iconic moments in Billie Jean King's career and the broader history of women's sports came in September 1973, when she faced former men's champion Bobby Riggs in a highly publicized exhibition match dubbed the "Battle of the Sexes." Riggs, a self-proclaimed chauvinist, had challenged the notion that women could compete with men in sports.

The match, held at the Houston Astrodome, captivated the nation and the world. It symbolized the broader struggle for gender equality during the women's liberation movement. Billie Jean King's victory over Bobby Riggs in straight sets demonstrated not only her exceptional skill but also the capability of female athletes to excel under the same pressure and scrutiny as their male counterparts.

Billie Jean King's triumph in the "Battle of the Sexes" had a profound impact, sparking conversations about gender equity not only in sports but also in society at large. Her advocacy efforts led to significant changes in women's tennis, including equal prize money at major tournaments and increased recognition and opportunities for female athletes.

Beyond her work in sports, King continued to be a leading advocate for gender and LGBTQ+ rights. She publicly came out as gay in 1981, becoming one of the first prominent athletes to do so. Her openness and activism paved the way for greater acceptance and inclusivity in the sports world.

Throughout her life, Billie Jean King has received numerous accolades and honors, including the Presidential Medal of Freedom. Her legacy as a sports pioneer, gender equality advocate, and LGBTQ+ rights activist continues to inspire athletes and advocates around the world. Billie Jean King's unwavering commitment to equality serves as a beacon of hope and a reminder that sports have the power to drive positive social change and break down barriers of discrimination and prejudice.

Serena Williams: Dominating Tennis and Advocating for Gender and Racial Equality

In the world of tennis, Serena Williams is an icon of athletic excellence and a powerful advocate for gender and racial equality. Her remarkable career has not only redefined the sport but also amplified the importance of diversity and inclusion, inspiring a new generation of athletes and advocates.

Serena Jameka Williams was born on September 26, 1981, in Saginaw, Michigan, and grew up in Compton, California. From a young age, Serena and her sister Venus showed prodigious talent on the tennis court. Under the guidance of their father, Richard Williams, the sisters embarked on a journey that would forever change the landscape of women's tennis.

Serena's ascent in the tennis world was swift and relentless. She turned professional in 1995, and by 1999, she had claimed her first Grand Slam title at the U.S. Open. Her powerful serves, fierce competitiveness, and unmatched athleticism made her a dominant force in the sport. Serena's total of 23 Grand Slam singles titles (as of my knowledge cutoff date in September 2021) is a testament to her enduring excellence and competitiveness.

As Serena's tennis career soared, she also embraced her role as an advocate for gender and racial equality. Throughout her career, she has been a vocal proponent of equal pay for female athletes and has raised awareness about the disparities that persist in sports. Her willingness to speak out on these issues, even in the face of criticism, has made her a leading voice in the fight for equity in sports.

Serena Williams's impact on diversity and inclusion in tennis and beyond is profound. Her success has shattered stereotypes and broken down barriers for Black athletes in a predominantly white sport. She has inspired countless young girls, particularly those from underrepresented communities, to pursue their dreams in tennis and other fields.

Beyond her advocacy for gender equity, Serena Williams has also been an outspoken advocate for racial justice. She has supported the Black Lives Matter movement and used her platform to raise awareness about issues of systemic racism and police brutality. Her commitment to social justice and racial equality reflects her understanding of the broader societal issues that transcend the world of sports.

Off the court, Serena has pursued entrepreneurial endeavors, including fashion and philanthropy. She established the Serena Williams Fund, which focuses on promoting equity and access in education. Her commitment to giving back to her community and addressing social issues aligns with her belief that athletes have a responsibility to effect positive change.

Throughout her career, Serena Williams has faced adversity, including injuries and personal challenges, but she has consistently displayed resilience and a relentless work ethic. Her ability to return to the top of the tennis world after setbacks is a testament to her character and determination.

Serena Williams's legacy extends far beyond the tennis court. She is an inspiration to athletes and advocates alike, demonstrating that one's platform can be used to effect meaningful change. Her advocacy for gender and racial equality has left an indelible mark on the sports world, prompting important conversations and driving progress. Serena Williams's impact on tennis, diversity, and social justice serves as a powerful reminder of the transformative potential of athletes who use their voices for positive change.

Mia Hamm: Inspiring a Generation as a Soccer Superstar and Two-Time Olympic Gold Medalist

In the world of soccer, Mia Hamm is synonymous with excellence, determination, and inspiring a generation of athletes, particularly young girls, to pursue their dreams in sports. Her remarkable career as a soccer superstar, coupled with her advocacy for gender equality in sports, has left an enduring legacy that transcends the boundaries of the soccer field.

Mia Hamm was born on March 17, 1972, in Selma, Alabama, and grew up in a military family, which meant frequent moves during her childhood. Despite these challenges, her love for soccer blossomed at an early age. Hamm's incredible talent and dedication quickly set her apart as a rising star in the sport.

Hamm's soccer journey took a significant step forward when she joined the U.S. women's national soccer team at the age of 15, becoming the youngest player ever to do so. Her rapid ascent continued when she attended the University of North Carolina, where she played a pivotal role in winning four consecutive NCAA championships.

At the international level, Mia Hamm's impact was profound. She represented the United States in four FIFA Women's World Cup tournaments and four Olympic Games. Her performances on the field were nothing short of spectacular, earning her recognition as one of the greatest female soccer players in history.

A defining moment in Mia Hamm's career came at the 1996 Atlanta Olympics when women's soccer was included for the first time. Hamm's exceptional skills and leadership were instrumental in leading the U.S. women's soccer team to a gold medal victory. This historic achievement not only showcased her talent but also helped elevate the popularity of women's soccer in the United States.

Over the course of her career, Mia Hamm amassed numerous accolades, including two Olympic gold medals and two FIFA Women's World Cup titles. She also became the all-time leading scorer in international women's soccer, a record that stood for many years.

Beyond her contributions on the field, Mia Hamm used her platform to advocate for gender equality in sports. She was a vocal supporter of Title IX, the federal law that prohibits sex-based discrimination in education and athletics. Hamm recognized the importance of providing equal opportunities for female athletes and worked tirelessly to promote gender equity in sports.

Hamm's influence extended to her philanthropic efforts. She co-founded the Mia Hamm Foundation, which focuses on empowering young girls and advancing research and treatment for rare diseases. Her commitment to giving back and using her platform to create positive change reflects her belief in the broader impact of sports.

In the years following her retirement from professional soccer, Mia Hamm's legacy continues to inspire generations of athletes, particularly young girls who aspire to follow in her footsteps. Her impact on the growth and development of women's soccer in the United States is immeasurable.

Mia Hamm's life and career serve as a testament to the transformative power of sports and the importance of advocating for gender equality in athletics. Her dedication to excellence on the field, her tireless efforts to advance opportunities for female athletes, and her commitment to making a positive impact in the community have solidified her legacy as an icon in both the world of sports and the broader arena of social change.

Chapter 17: Female Leaders in Business and Politics

Indra Nooyi: Leading PepsiCo as CEO and Reshaping the Food and Beverage Industry

In the corporate world, few leaders have left as indelible a mark as Indra Nooyi, the former CEO of PepsiCo. Her trailblazing career, marked by strategic innovation and a commitment to sustainability, has not only transformed one of the world's largest food and beverage companies but has also set an inspiring example for women aspiring to leadership roles in business and politics.

Indra Krishnamurthy Nooyi was born on October 28, 1955, in Chennai, India. She demonstrated exceptional academic prowess from an early age, earning a bachelor's degree in physics, chemistry, and mathematics from Madras Christian College and a master's degree in business administration from the Indian Institute of Management Calcutta. Her educational achievements set the stage for a remarkable career.

Nooyi's journey in the corporate world began when she joined Boston Consulting Group, a global management consulting firm. Her analytical skills and strategic acumen quickly earned her recognition, and she was later appointed as a senior vice president and director of corporate strategy and planning at Motorola.

However, it was her tenure at PepsiCo that would become the defining chapter of her career. Nooyi joined PepsiCo in 1994 and steadily climbed the corporate ladder. In 2006, she reached the pinnacle of success when she was named the CEO of the company, becoming one of the few women of color to lead a Fortune 500 company.

Under Nooyi's leadership, PepsiCo underwent a remarkable transformation. She championed a shift toward healthier products and sustainability, recognizing the changing preferences of consumers and the importance of environmental responsibility. This strategic pivot led to innovations such as the acquisition of brands like Tropicana and Quaker Oats, positioning PepsiCo as a leader in the health and wellness sector.

One of Indra Nooyi's enduring legacies at PepsiCo was her commitment to diversity and inclusion. She advocated for the development and advancement of women and underrepresented minorities within the company's ranks, leading to a more inclusive corporate culture.

Nooyi's advocacy for sustainability was equally impactful. Under her guidance, PepsiCo implemented sustainability initiatives that aimed to reduce the company's environmental footprint. These efforts included commitments to water conservation, waste reduction, and responsible sourcing of ingredients.

Nooyi's tenure as CEO of PepsiCo was marked by numerous accolades, including being named to Forbes' list of the world's 100 most powerful women multiple times. Her leadership, both in the boardroom and on the global stage, made her a prominent figure in business and politics.

Beyond her corporate accomplishments, Indra Nooyi's influence extended to her advocacy for women's leadership and her involvement in policy discussions on issues such as corporate governance and sustainability. She has served on the boards of several prestigious organizations and institutions, further cementing her reputation as a thought leader and influencer.

Indra Nooyi's retirement from PepsiCo in 2018 marked the end of an era, but her impact continues to resonate. Her legacy is a testament to the power of leadership, innovation, and a commitment to values that extend beyond the bottom line. Indra Nooyi's remarkable journey from India to the pinnacle of the corporate world serves as an inspiration for aspiring leaders, particularly women, who seek to make a positive impact in business and politics.

Margaret Thatcher: Becoming the UK's First Female Prime Minister and a Global Political Icon

Margaret Thatcher, known as the "Iron Lady," will forever be remembered as a trailblazer in the world of politics and a transformative figure in British history. Her rise to become the United Kingdom's first female Prime Minister and her unwavering commitment to conservative principles left an indelible mark on the global political landscape.

Margaret Hilda Roberts was born on October 13, 1925, in Grantham, Lincolnshire, England. Her early life was marked by modesty and determination. She excelled academically and studied chemistry at the University of Oxford, where she developed her critical thinking and leadership skills.

Thatcher's entry into politics came in 1959 when she was elected as the Member of Parliament (MP) for Finchley. Her early years in Parliament were marked by her outspokenness and dedication to conservative values. She quickly gained recognition as a rising star within the Conservative Party.

In 1975, Thatcher made history when she was elected as the leader of the Conservative Party, becoming the first woman to lead a major political party in the United Kingdom. Her leadership style was characterized by a resolute commitment to her principles, earning her the nickname "Iron Lady." Her vision for a more market-oriented and economically conservative Britain resonated with many.

In 1979, Margaret Thatcher's political journey reached its zenith when she was elected as the Prime Minister of the United Kingdom. She inherited a nation grappling with economic challenges, including high inflation and unemployment. Thatcher's leadership was defined by her unwavering commitment to economic reform and her resolve to reduce the power of trade unions.

Thatcher's government implemented a series of controversial policies known as "Thatcherism." These policies included privatization of state-owned industries, deregulation, and a commitment to free-market economics. While they sparked intense debates and protests, they also contributed to a transformation of the British economy.

One of the defining moments of Margaret Thatcher's leadership came during the Falklands War in 1982. Her resolute decision to retake the Falkland Islands from Argentine forces earned her widespread support and bolstered her reputation as a strong and decisive leader.

Internationally, Thatcher was a prominent figure in the global political arena. Her close relationship with U.S. President Ronald Reagan, with whom she shared conservative values, shaped the direction of Western policy during the Cold War. Together, they championed free-market capitalism and took a hardline stance against the Soviet Union.

Thatcher's tenure as Prime Minister was marked by both accomplishments and controversies. Her policies spurred economic growth but also led to social upheaval and political divisions. Her leadership style was often polarizing, with passionate supporters and critics alike.

In 1990, after more than a decade in office, Margaret Thatcher stepped down as Prime Minister. Her resignation marked the end of an era in British politics, but her legacy endured. She continued to serve as a Member of Parliament until her retirement in 1992.

Margaret Thatcher's impact on the world of politics extended far beyond her time in office. She remains an iconic figure in conservative and political circles, admired for her strength, conviction, and pioneering spirit. Her legacy as the first female Prime Minister of the United Kingdom and a global political icon serves as an inspiration for women in politics and leadership worldwide. Margaret Thatcher's life and career remind us of the enduring impact that determined and principled leaders can have on the course of history.

Condoleezza Rice: Breaking Barriers as the First African American Woman to Serve as U.S. Secretary of State

Condoleezza Rice's ascent to become the 66th U.S. Secretary of State marked a historic milestone in American politics. As the first African American woman to hold this prestigious position, Rice shattered barriers and became a trailblazer in the realms of diplomacy and national security, leaving an enduring legacy of leadership and public service.

Condoleezza Rice was born on November 14, 1954, in Birmingham, Alabama. Her early life was deeply influenced by the civil rights movement and the racial segregation of the American South. Despite these challenges, Rice's parents instilled in her a love for education and a strong work ethic.

Rice's academic achievements set her on a path to excellence. She earned a bachelor's degree in political science from the University of Denver, followed by a master's degree from the University of Notre Dame and a Ph.D. in political science from the University of Denver. Her academic pursuits and passion for international relations laid the foundation for her future career in foreign policy.

Rice's journey in politics began when she joined the administration of President George H.W. Bush in the late 1980s. She served as a specialist on the Soviet Union and Eastern Europe on the National Security Council and later as the Special Assistant to the President for National Security Affairs. Her expertise in international affairs quickly became evident to those around her.

However, it was during the administration of President George W. Bush that Rice's career reached its pinnacle. In 2001, she was appointed as the National Security Advisor, becoming the first woman to hold this position. In this role, she played a critical role in shaping the United States' response to the 9/11 terrorist attacks and in formulating national security policy.

Rice's most historic appointment came in 2005 when she was nominated by President George W. Bush to serve as the U.S. Secretary of State, succeeding Colin Powell. Her confirmation made her the first African American woman and the second woman ever to hold this prestigious office.

As Secretary of State, Condoleezza Rice played a central role in American foreign policy during a pivotal period in history. She faced numerous challenges, including the wars in Iraq and Afghanistan, efforts to combat terrorism, and the promotion of democracy and human rights worldwide. Her leadership and diplomatic skills were put to the test on the global stage.

One of Rice's enduring legacies as Secretary of State was her commitment to diplomacy and engagement with the international community. She emphasized the importance of alliances and partnerships in addressing global challenges, a stance that sought to rebuild relationships after periods of strain.

After leaving office in 2009, Rice returned to academia and public service. She continued to be a respected voice on foreign policy and international affairs, authoring books and serving on various boards and commissions.

Condoleezza Rice's remarkable journey from a racially segregated Birmingham to becoming the U.S. Secretary of State exemplifies the American dream and the power of education, determination, and leadership. Her historic appointment as the first African American woman to hold this position represents a significant milestone in the annals of American politics and diplomacy. Rice's legacy as a trailblazer, diplomat, and advocate for global engagement underscores the profound impact that individuals can have on shaping the course of history and advancing the cause of equality and leadership.

Chapter 18: Women in Medicine and Healthcare

Florence Nightingale: Revolutionizing Nursing Care and Epidemiology

Florence Nightingale, known as the "Lady with the Lamp," is celebrated not only for her pioneering work in nursing care but also for her profound impact on healthcare and epidemiology. Her unwavering dedication to improving the conditions of hospitals and her innovative approaches to healthcare have left an enduring legacy in the field of medicine.

Florence Nightingale was born on May 12, 1820, in Florence, Italy, and raised in England. From a young age, she displayed a deep interest in nursing and healthcare, defying societal norms that expected women of her social class to pursue traditional roles. Her determination to make a difference in healthcare became evident as she embarked on her journey.

In 1854, Florence Nightingale and a team of nurses were sent to the Crimean War to tend to wounded British soldiers. The conditions in military hospitals at the time were deplorable, with high mortality rates due to disease and poor sanitation. Nightingale's leadership and commitment to patient care transformed these hospitals.

One of Nightingale's most notable contributions was her emphasis on sanitation and hygiene. She implemented rigorous handwashing practices, maintained clean and well-ventilated hospital wards, and advocated for proper waste disposal. Her efforts significantly reduced the spread of infections, ultimately saving countless lives.

Nightingale's compassion and dedication earned her the nickname "the Lady with the Lamp." She would make nightly rounds through the hospital, providing comfort and care to wounded soldiers. Her presence became a symbol of hope and compassion during a time of great suffering.

After the Crimean War, Florence Nightingale continued her work in healthcare reform and nursing education. She founded the Nightingale School of Nursing at St. Thomas' Hospital in London, setting high standards for nursing education and practice. Her writings, including the influential "Notes on Nursing," became essential texts for nurses worldwide.

Beyond her work in nursing, Florence Nightingale made significant contributions to epidemiology, the study of disease patterns. She was a pioneer in collecting and analyzing healthcare data, using statistics to track disease outbreaks and improve public health. Her work on hospital design and management laid the foundation for modern healthcare systems.

Florence Nightingale's impact extended far beyond her lifetime. Her dedication to nursing and healthcare reform revolutionized the field, emphasizing the importance of patient care, hygiene, and evidence-based practices. Her legacy continues to inspire nurses and healthcare professionals around the world.

Nightingale's commitment to the well-being of patients and her innovative approaches to healthcare have left an indelible mark on medicine. Her work serves as a reminder of the transformative power of one individual's passion, compassion, and determination in improving the lives of others. Florence Nightingale's legacy is not only a testament to her pioneering spirit but also a beacon of inspiration for all those who strive to make a positive impact in healthcare and medicine.

Elizabeth Blackwell: Becoming the First Woman to Receive a Medical Degree in the United States

Elizabeth Blackwell's journey to becoming the first woman in the United States to earn a medical degree is a testament to her perseverance, courage, and determination to break down gender barriers in the field of medicine. Her pioneering achievements not only opened doors for women in healthcare but also challenged societal norms and transformed the landscape of medical education.

Elizabeth Blackwell was born on February 3, 1821, in Bristol, England, and grew up in a family that prioritized education and social reform. Her father, Samuel Blackwell, was a progressive thinker who believed in equal education for his daughters. These early values would play a significant role in shaping Elizabeth's future.

In 1832, the Blackwell family relocated to the United States. Tragedy struck the family when Elizabeth's father passed away, leaving them in financial hardship. Despite the challenges, Elizabeth and her sisters continued their education with the support of their mother and a local schoolteacher.

Inspired by a family friend who was suffering from a terminal illness and believed that a female physician would have provided more compassionate care, Elizabeth Blackwell resolved to pursue a career in medicine. However, the path to medical school was filled with obstacles, primarily because no medical school in the United States admitted women at the time.

Undeterred by the prevailing gender biases, Blackwell persevered in her quest for education. She applied to numerous medical schools and faced rejection after rejection. Her determination paid off when she was accepted to Geneva Medical College in Geneva, New York, in 1847.

Elizabeth Blackwell's journey at Geneva Medical College was challenging. She faced hostility and discrimination from both students and faculty, many of whom did not want a woman in their ranks. However, she persevered, excelled in her studies, and graduated in 1849 with her medical degree, becoming the first woman to achieve this feat in the United States.

After graduation, Blackwell continued to break down barriers. She went to Europe for further medical training and gained valuable experience in hospitals in London and Paris. Upon her return to the United States, she faced resistance when seeking employment as a physician. Nevertheless, she was determined to provide healthcare to underserved populations.

In 1857, Elizabeth Blackwell, along with her sister Emily Blackwell and Dr. Marie Zakrzewska, co-founded the New York Infirmary for Indigent Women and Children, a hospital that provided medical care to the poor and served as a teaching institution for women in medicine. This marked a significant step forward in women's access to medical education and practice.

Throughout her life, Blackwell advocated for women's rights and health issues. She believed that women's unique perspectives and skills could contribute to improvements in healthcare and society at large. Her writings, including "The Laws of Life with Special Reference to the Physical Education of Girls," reflected her progressive views on women's health and education.

Elizabeth Blackwell's pioneering achievements paved the way for generations of women to enter the medical profession. Her legacy as the first American woman to earn a medical degree stands as a testament to her courage and resilience in the face of adversity. She not only shattered gender barriers but also left an indelible mark on the field of medicine, reminding us of the transformative power of determination and the pursuit of equality in education and healthcare.

Helen Brooke Taussig: Pioneering Pediatric Cardiology and Advancing Open-Heart Surgery for Children

Helen Brooke Taussig, a trailblazing American cardiologist, is celebrated for her groundbreaking work in pediatric cardiology, particularly her contributions to the development of open-heart surgery for children with congenital heart defects. Her dedication to improving the lives of young patients and her innovative approaches to cardiac care have had a profound and lasting impact on the field of medicine.

Helen Brooke Taussig was born on May 24, 1898, in Cambridge, Massachusetts. She grew up in a family of intellectuals and educators, which fostered her early love for learning and science. Despite facing challenges related to hearing impairment, Taussig was determined to pursue a career in medicine.

After completing her undergraduate studies at Radcliffe College, Taussig enrolled at Harvard Medical School, where she became one of the first female students. Her medical education was marked by exceptional dedication and a commitment to understanding congenital heart conditions, which had limited treatment options at the time.

Taussig's breakthrough moment came in the 1940s when she began collaborating with surgeon Alfred Blalock and surgical technician Vivien Thomas at Johns Hopkins University. Together, they embarked on a mission to address congenital heart defects, which were often considered untreatable in children.

One of the most significant contributions of this team was the development of the Blalock-Taussig shunt, a surgical procedure that created an artificial connection between the pulmonary artery and the aorta to improve blood flow. This innovation, introduced in 1944, was a groundbreaking step in the treatment of congenital heart conditions, specifically the "blue baby syndrome."

The Blalock-Taussig shunt procedure allowed children with congenital heart defects to survive beyond infancy and paved the way for subsequent advances in pediatric cardiac surgery. It represented a turning point in the field of pediatric cardiology and earned Taussig international recognition.

Helen Brooke Taussig's work extended beyond surgical innovations. She was instrumental in establishing the field of pediatric cardiology as a distinct medical specialty. Her dedication to the care and well-being of young patients, coupled with her tireless advocacy for improved treatment options, elevated the standards of pediatric cardiac care worldwide.

In 1954, Taussig's contributions were further recognized when she became the first woman to serve as the president of the American Heart Association. Her leadership and advocacy continued to shape the landscape of cardiovascular medicine, emphasizing the importance of early detection and intervention in congenital heart conditions.

Throughout her career, Helen Brooke Taussig remained committed to patient care, research, and education. She trained numerous physicians in the specialized field of pediatric cardiology, ensuring that her legacy would be carried forward by future generations of medical professionals.

Taussig's pioneering spirit, dedication, and groundbreaking innovations have had a profound and lasting impact on the field of medicine. Her work not only saved countless lives but also transformed the way congenital heart defects are diagnosed and treated. Helen Brooke Taussig's legacy serves as an enduring inspiration for medical professionals and a testament to the transformative power of dedication and innovation in the pursuit of improved healthcare for all, especially the most vulnerable among us—children.

Virginia Apgar: Developing the Apgar Score for Newborns and Advancing Neonatology

Virginia Apgar, a pioneering American physician, is renowned for her groundbreaking contributions to the field of neonatology and her development of the Apgar Score, a simple yet revolutionary tool used worldwide to assess the health of newborns immediately after birth. Her dedication to improving the care of newborns and her innovative approach to medical assessment have saved countless lives and left an indelible mark on the field of medicine.

Virginia Apgar was born on June 7, 1909, in Westfield, New Jersey. Her early fascination with science and biology, coupled with a strong academic aptitude, paved the way for her career in medicine. After completing her undergraduate studies at Mount Holyoke College, she attended the College of Physicians and Surgeons at Columbia University, where she earned her medical degree in 1933.

Apgar's journey in neonatology and perinatal medicine began during her residency at Columbia-Presbyterian Medical Center, where she was exposed to the challenges and critical needs of newborns. This experience ignited her passion for improving neonatal care and led her to pursue further studies in anesthesia.

In 1952, Apgar introduced the world to the Apgar Score, a systematic and quick assessment tool to evaluate the physical condition of newborns immediately after birth. The Apgar Score, which assesses five vital signs—Appearance, Pulse, Grimace, Activity, and Respiration—provides a numerical score between 0 and 10, with higher scores indicating better health. This straightforward assessment allowed medical professionals to quickly identify newborns in need of immediate medical attention.

The introduction of the Apgar Score revolutionized the care of newborns and greatly improved their chances of survival. It enabled medical teams to make rapid decisions about interventions and treatments, ensuring that newborns received timely and appropriate care. The Apgar Score remains a fundamental tool in neonatal medicine and has saved countless lives by facilitating early intervention.

Virginia Apgar's commitment to neonatology extended beyond the development of the Apgar Score. She conducted pioneering research on the effects of anesthesia on newborns and made significant contributions to the understanding of neonatal jaundice. Her work helped shape the field of perinatal medicine and laid the foundation for further advances in neonatal care.

Throughout her career, Apgar advocated for increased awareness of the importance of neonatal health and the critical role of medical professionals in caring for newborns. She also worked to improve medical education, particularly in the area of anesthesia.

In recognition of her groundbreaking contributions, Virginia Apgar received numerous awards and honors, including the establishment of the Virginia Apgar Award by the American Academy of Pediatrics. Her legacy endures not only through the Apgar Score but also through the countless lives she touched and the generations of healthcare professionals she inspired.

Virginia Apgar's pioneering spirit, dedication to newborns, and innovative approach to medical assessment have had a profound and lasting impact on the field of medicine. Her work has saved countless lives and continues to be a cornerstone of neonatal care. Virginia Apgar's legacy serves as an enduring inspiration for medical professionals and a testament to the transformative power of innovation and dedication in the pursuit of improved healthcare for the most vulnerable among us—newborns.

Chapter 19: Women in Entertainment and Pop Culture

Audrey Hepburn: Shining as an Iconic Actress and Humanitarian

Audrey Hepburn, the epitome of elegance and grace, is celebrated not only for her iconic performances as an actress but also for her remarkable humanitarian work. Her enduring legacy extends from the silver screen to her tireless efforts to improve the lives of children around the world, making her a beloved figure in both entertainment and philanthropy.

Audrey Hepburn was born on May 4, 1929, in Brussels, Belgium. Her early life was marked by the challenges of World War II, during which she and her family faced hardships and the occupation of their homeland by Nazi forces. These formative experiences instilled in her a deep sense of compassion and a desire to make a positive impact on the world.

Hepburn's journey in the world of entertainment began in ballet, where she initially aspired to become a professional dancer. Her exquisite beauty and undeniable talent caught the attention of casting directors, leading her to make her film debut in the 1951 British film "The Lavender Hill Mob." This marked the beginning of her iconic career in acting.

One of Hepburn's most memorable roles came in 1953 when she starred as Princess Ann in "Roman Holiday." The film catapulted her to international stardom and earned her an Academy Award for Best Actress. Her performance was lauded for its charm and vulnerability, qualities that would become synonymous with Hepburn's on-screen persona.

Audrey Hepburn's career continued to flourish with roles in classic films such as "Breakfast at Tiffany's," "My Fair Lady," and "Sabrina." Her elegance, style, and charisma made her a beloved figure in Hollywood and an enduring fashion icon. Hepburn's influence on the world of fashion is still felt today, with her timeless wardrobe choices setting enduring trends.

While Hepburn's contributions to entertainment were undoubtedly significant, it was her humanitarian work that cemented her legacy as a remarkable woman of compassion and dedication. Her experiences during World War II and her own struggles with malnutrition as a child deeply impacted her perspective on the plight of vulnerable children.

In 1988, Audrey Hepburn became a Goodwill Ambassador for UNICEF, the United Nations Children's Fund. Her work with UNICEF took her to some of the most impoverished and war-torn regions of the world, where she witnessed the suffering of children firsthand. Her advocacy focused on providing life-saving aid, including food, clean water, and healthcare, to children in need.

Hepburn's dedication to UNICEF was unwavering, and she used her platform to raise awareness and funds for the organization's critical work. She became a voice for the voiceless and a tireless advocate for children's rights. Her efforts helped improve the lives of countless children around the world, and she received the Presidential Medal of Freedom in recognition of her humanitarian contributions.

Audrey Hepburn's life and career serve as an inspiration for aspiring actors and humanitarians alike. Her ability to transition seamlessly between the worlds of entertainment and philanthropy demonstrates the transformative power of fame when used for the greater good. Hepburn's enduring legacy reminds us that compassion, grace, and a commitment to making the world a better place can leave an indelible mark on the hearts of millions and serve as a beacon of hope for future generations.

Lucille Ball: Redefining Comedy and Breaking Gender Barriers in Television

Lucille Ball, often regarded as one of the greatest comedians in television history, not only redefined the landscape of comedy but also shattered gender barriers in the entertainment industry. Her wit, talent, and pioneering spirit made her a beloved and influential figure whose legacy continues to shape the world of entertainment.

Lucille Ball was born on August 6, 1911, in Jamestown, New York. From an early age, she displayed a natural talent for performing and a penchant for making people laugh. These early inclinations would set the stage for her remarkable career in comedy.

Ball's journey in entertainment began with modeling and work in B-movies. However, her big break came when she was cast as the scatterbrained housewife Lucy Ricardo in the groundbreaking television series "I Love Lucy." Premiering in 1951, the show quickly became a cultural phenomenon and catapulted Ball to stardom.

"I Love Lucy" was revolutionary in many ways. It was one of the first television programs to be filmed in front of a live studio audience, and it introduced the concept of reruns, which allowed a wider audience to enjoy the show. Ball's portrayal of Lucy Ricardo, a character known for her comedic antics and misadventures, endeared her to viewers across the nation.

What made Lucille Ball's role particularly groundbreaking was her status as both the star and executive producer of "I Love Lucy." Alongside her husband, Desi Arnaz, she formed Desilu Productions, becoming one of the first women to head a major Hollywood studio. This bold move gave her creative control and financial independence in an industry where women in leadership roles were rare.

Ball's success went beyond her work in front of the camera. She was a trailblazer in television production, using her influence to champion innovative ideas and introduce technologies that would later become industry standards. Under her guidance, Desilu Productions pioneered the use of multiple cameras, live audiences, and the concept of syndication.

Moreover, Ball's contributions to the television industry extended to her groundbreaking decision to incorporate her real-life pregnancy into the storyline of "I Love Lucy." This was a daring move at the time, challenging societal norms and taboos regarding pregnancy on television. The episode in which Lucy gives birth to Little Ricky remains one of the most-watched and beloved moments in television history.

Lucille Ball's legacy as a comedy icon and trailblazing producer continues to influence comedians, actors, and producers to this day. Her impact on gender equality in Hollywood and her ability to navigate the male-dominated entertainment industry set a precedent for future generations of women in show business.

In recognition of her contributions, Lucille Ball received numerous accolades, including multiple Emmy Awards and a Lifetime Achievement Award from the Kennedy Center Honors. Her influence on comedy and her role in breaking down gender barriers in television remain a testament to her enduring legacy.

Lucille Ball's ability to make audiences laugh, challenge societal norms, and pave the way for female leaders in entertainment has left an indelible mark on the world of comedy and television. Her work continues to inspire and entertain, proving that humor and courage can transcend time and generations, leaving a lasting impact on the art of entertainment.

Marilyn Monroe: Captivating Hollywood and Becoming a Timeless Cultural Icon

Marilyn Monroe, the epitome of Hollywood glamour and sensuality, is celebrated not only for her iconic beauty but also for her enduring status as a cultural icon. Her life, career, and enigmatic persona continue to fascinate and inspire generations of fans worldwide.

Marilyn Monroe was born as Norma Jeane Mortenson on June 1, 1926, in Los Angeles, California. Her early life was marked by instability and adversity, including time spent in foster care and orphanages. Despite these challenges, she possessed a natural talent for modeling and acting, which she pursued as a means to escape her difficult circumstances.

Monroe's breakthrough in Hollywood came in the early 1950s when she signed a contract with 20th Century Fox and adopted her famous stage name, Marilyn Monroe. Her platinum blonde hair, captivating smile, and hourglass figure made her an instant sensation in an era dominated by classic Hollywood stars.

One of Monroe's most iconic roles came in Billy Wilder's 1955 film "The Seven Year Itch," where she famously stood over a subway grate as her white dress billowed up. The image became an enduring symbol of Monroe's allure and is one of the most recognized moments in cinematic history.

Monroe's performances in films like "Gentlemen Prefer Blondes," "Some Like It Hot," and "How to Marry a Millionaire" solidified her status as a beloved and bankable movie star. Her comedic talent, combined with her undeniable charisma, endeared her to audiences worldwide.

Beyond her film career, Monroe was known for her tumultuous personal life and complex persona. Her marriages to baseball legend Joe DiMaggio and playwright Arthur Miller garnered significant media attention. Her vulnerability and struggles with mental health added depth to her public image, and she became an unwitting symbol of the pressures and challenges faced by Hollywood stars.

Tragically, Marilyn Monroe's life was cut short when she died on August 5, 1962, at the age of 36. Her death, officially ruled as a probable suicide, has been the subject of speculation and conspiracy theories, further adding to her mystique.

Despite her relatively brief career and turbulent personal life, Marilyn Monroe's influence on popular culture remains profound. Her image and legacy have endured through the decades, and she remains an iconic symbol of beauty, sensuality, and female empowerment. Monroe's impact is seen in countless films, music, fashion, and art inspired by her timeless allure.

In recent years, Monroe's enduring legacy has been celebrated through retrospectives, exhibitions, and academic studies exploring her significance in American culture. Her contributions to film, fashion, and the art of celebrity have left an indelible mark on the entertainment industry, reminding us that the allure of Marilyn Monroe is not bound by time but continues to captivate and inspire audiences around the world.

Whitney Houston: Achieving Legendary Status with Her Powerful Voice and Music

Whitney Houston, often referred to as "The Voice," is celebrated as one of the greatest and most influential vocalists in music history. Her extraordinary talent, chart-topping hits, and unforgettable performances propelled her to legendary status, making her a beloved figure whose impact on the music industry and culture endures.

Whitney Elizabeth Houston was born on August 9, 1963, in Newark, New Jersey, into a musical family. Her mother, Cissy Houston, was a renowned gospel and R&B singer, and her cousin, Dionne Warwick, was a prominent vocalist. Whitney's upbringing in a family with deep musical roots laid the foundation for her future success.

Houston's journey in the music industry began in gospel choirs and nightclubs in New York City, where she showcased her remarkable vocal range and versatility. In 1983, she signed a record deal with Arista Records, marking the beginning of her meteoric rise to stardom.

Her self-titled debut album, released in 1985, catapulted Whitney Houston to fame. The album included hits like "Greatest Love of All" and "Saving All My Love for You," both of which showcased her incredible vocal prowess and earned her Grammy Awards. The album's unprecedented success made her a household name and established her as a force to be reckoned with in the music industry.

Houston's impact continued to grow with subsequent albums, including "Whitney" (1987), which featured chart-toppers like "I Wanna Dance with Somebody (Who Loves Me)," and "I'm Your Baby Tonight" (1990). Her soaring voice and emotive delivery made her a dominant presence on radio airwaves and music charts throughout the late 1980s and early 1990s.

In addition to her music career, Whitney Houston ventured into acting, starring in films such as "The Bodyguard" (1992) alongside Kevin Costner. The film's soundtrack featured the iconic ballad "I Will Always Love You," which became one of the best-selling singles of all time. Houston's portrayal of a pop star-turned-bodyguard's client solidified her status as a cultural icon.

Whitney Houston's vocal talent and stage presence were unparalleled. Her live performances, including the unforgettable rendition of the national anthem at Super Bowl XXV in 1991, were showcases of her vocal prowess and left audiences in awe.

Despite her incredible success, Houston faced personal challenges and struggles with substance abuse, which impacted her career and personal life. Tragically, on February 11, 2012, Whitney Houston passed away at the age of 48. Her untimely death marked the loss of a musical legend whose influence and contributions to the world of music continue to be celebrated.

Houston's impact on the music industry transcends generations, and her music remains a staple of radio playlists and streaming platforms. Her powerful voice, emotional depth, and timeless hits continue to inspire and resonate with fans worldwide. Whitney Houston's legacy as "The Voice" endures as a testament to the transcendent power of music and the indelible mark left by one of the greatest vocalists in history.

Chapter 20: Women in Philosophy and Thought

Simone de Beauvoir: Pioneering Feminist Philosophy with "The Second Sex"

Simone de Beauvoir, a French existentialist philosopher, writer, and feminist, is renowned for her groundbreaking work in philosophy and her seminal book, "The Second Sex." Her intellectual contributions revolutionized feminist thought and continue to shape discussions on gender, existentialism, and human existence.

Simone de Beauvoir was born on January 9, 1908, in Paris, France. Her early exposure to literature and philosophy, coupled with her keen intellect, set the stage for her future as a pioneering thinker. De Beauvoir pursued higher education at the Sorbonne, where she studied philosophy and met Jean-Paul Sartre, with whom she would develop a profound intellectual and personal partnership.

De Beauvoir and Sartre's philosophical exploration of existentialism, which emphasizes individual freedom, choice, and responsibility, deeply influenced her work. Her philosophical inquiries extended to questions of gender and feminism, marking a significant departure from traditional existentialist thought.

In 1949, Simone de Beauvoir published her magnum opus, "The Second Sex" ("Le Deuxième Sexe" in French). This monumental work is considered a foundational text in feminist philosophy and remains a cornerstone of feminist literature. "The Second Sex" critically examined the social, cultural, and historical construction of femininity and the ways in which women had been relegated to a secondary, or "other," status in society.

One of the central themes of "The Second Sex" is the concept of "The Other," which de Beauvoir argued was a construct used to oppress women and define them in relation to men. She explored how women's roles, identities, and experiences had been defined by patriarchal norms, and she called for a radical reevaluation of the relationship between the sexes.

De Beauvoir's work also challenged conventional notions of femininity and advocated for women's agency and self-determination. She famously declared, "One is not born, but rather becomes, a woman," emphasizing that gender identity is not predetermined but constructed through social and cultural influences.

"The Second Sex" sparked controversy and debate upon its release but quickly gained recognition as a seminal work in feminist philosophy. It inspired subsequent generations of feminist thinkers, activists, and scholars, including those involved in the women's liberation movement of the 1960s and 1970s.

Simone de Beauvoir's influence extended beyond the realm of philosophy and feminism. She was a prolific writer, producing novels, essays, and memoirs that explored existentialist themes, the complexities of human relationships, and the search for meaning in a world marked by ambiguity.

Throughout her life, de Beauvoir remained an outspoken advocate for women's rights and social justice. Her work laid the intellectual groundwork for feminist movements around the world and continues to inform contemporary discussions on gender equality, women's liberation, and the intersection of philosophy and feminism.

Simone de Beauvoir's intellectual contributions and unwavering commitment to challenging societal norms and gender inequality have left an indelible mark on the fields of philosophy and feminism. Her legacy as a pioneering feminist philosopher and writer serves as a testament to the enduring power of ideas in reshaping our understanding of human existence and the quest for equality and justice.

Hypatia of Alexandria: Advancing Mathematics and Philosophy in Ancient Greece

Hypatia of Alexandria, a remarkable scholar and philosopher who lived in the late 4th and early 5th centuries CE, is celebrated for her contributions to mathematics, philosophy, and the promotion of knowledge in a tumultuous period of history. Her pioneering work in mathematics and her dedication to philosophical inquiry made her a luminary figure in the intellectual circles of ancient Greece and a symbol of scholarship and reason.

Born around 360 CE in Alexandria, Egypt, Hypatia was the daughter of Theon of Alexandria, a prominent mathematician and philosopher who recognized and nurtured her exceptional intellectual abilities. Under her father's guidance, Hypatia received a comprehensive education that included mathematics, philosophy, astronomy, and literature.

Hypatia's expertise in mathematics was particularly noteworthy. She made significant contributions to algebra, geometry, and number theory, and she was known for her commentaries on the works of renowned mathematicians like Euclid and Ptolemy. Her mathematical teachings and writings played a crucial role in preserving and transmitting mathematical knowledge from antiquity to the Middle Ages.

In addition to her mathematical pursuits, Hypatia was a prominent philosopher and a proponent of Neoplatonism, a philosophical system that blended elements of Platonic thought with various mystical and metaphysical ideas. She delivered public lectures and engaged in philosophical debates, attracting students and intellectuals from across the Mediterranean region to study under her tutelage.

Hypatia's influence extended beyond her academic achievements. She became a symbol of intellectual independence and rational inquiry in a society marked by religious and political tensions. During her lifetime, Alexandria was a cosmopolitan city with a diverse population, but it was also a place of conflict between religious sects, including Christians and pagans.

Tragically, Hypatia's life was cut short by a horrific incident in 415 CE. Amidst the religious tensions of the time, she was brutally murdered by a mob of religious extremists, marking a dark chapter in the history of intellectual freedom.

Hypatia's legacy, however, endures. Her contributions to mathematics and philosophy left an indelible mark on the history of ideas, and she continues to be celebrated as an emblem of intellectual curiosity, independence, and resilience. Her story also serves as a poignant reminder of the enduring struggle for knowledge, reason, and tolerance in the face of intolerance and ignorance.

In modern times, Hypatia is revered as a trailblazer for women in science and philosophy, and her name is synonymous with the pursuit of knowledge and the enduring power of education. Her life and work continue to inspire scholars, scientists, and advocates for intellectual freedom, reinforcing the importance of preserving and promoting the pursuit of truth and wisdom in all societies.

Ayn Rand: Shaping Objectivism and Philosophical Thought with Novels Like "Atlas Shrugged"

Ayn Rand, a Russian-American novelist and philosopher, is celebrated for her distinctive philosophical system known as Objectivism and for her influential novels, including "Atlas Shrugged" and "The Fountainhead." Her ideas have left a lasting imprint on the fields of ethics, politics, and individualism, and her works continue to spark debate and discussion.

Ayn Rand was born Alisa Zinovyevna Rosenbaum on February 2, 1905, in St. Petersburg, Russia. Her early years were marked by the turmoil of the Russian Revolution, which she viewed as a tragic event that resulted in the loss of individual freedoms and the rise of collectivism. These experiences deeply influenced her philosophical outlook.

In 1926, Rand emigrated to the United States, where she pursued a career as a writer and philosopher. Her first major literary success came with the publication of "The Fountainhead" in 1943. The novel, which tells the story of an uncompromising architect named Howard Roark, explores themes of individualism, integrity, and the creative spirit. "The Fountainhead" gained a dedicated following and established Rand as a prominent writer.

However, it was her magnum opus, "Atlas Shrugged," published in 1957, that solidified Ayn Rand's reputation as a major intellectual figure. This monumental novel presents a dystopian vision of a society in decline, where government intervention and collectivism have stifled individual innovation and achievement. "Atlas Shrugged" introduced readers to Rand's philosophical system, Objectivism, which she defined as a philosophy of reason, individualism, and laissez-faire capitalism.

Objectivism, as outlined by Rand, emphasizes the importance of reason as the only means of gaining knowledge and making ethical decisions. It champions individual rights, personal responsibility, and rational self-interest as moral virtues. Rand's philosophy is a rejection of altruism and collectivism, advocating for the pursuit of one's own happiness and values as the highest moral purpose.

Ayn Rand's ideas and novels have inspired a dedicated following of Objectivists and libertarian thinkers. Her works, including "The Virtue of Selfishness" and "Capitalism: The Unknown Ideal," further expound upon her philosophical principles and their applications to ethics, politics, and economics.

While Rand's ideas have garnered both fervent support and staunch criticism, there is no denying her impact on contemporary political and philosophical discourse. Her advocacy for individualism and limited government intervention has influenced libertarian and conservative thought, while her novels have captured the imagination of readers worldwide.

Ayn Rand passed away on March 6, 1982, but her legacy endures through her writings and the continued discussions surrounding her ideas. Her commitment to the primacy of the individual, the importance of reason, and the defense of capitalism continues to shape debates on the role of government, the nature of morality, and the pursuit of individual happiness in a complex and ever-changing world.

Bell Hooks: Influential Feminist and Cultural Critic Exploring Race, Class, and Gender

Bell Hooks, a renowned feminist scholar, cultural critic, and author, has played a pivotal role in advancing feminist theory and critical studies on race, class, and gender. Her insightful writings, spanning numerous books and essays, have contributed to a deeper understanding of the intersections of oppression and the importance of intersectional feminism.

Born Gloria Jean Watkins on September 25, 1952, in Hopkinsville, Kentucky, Hooks adopted her pen name, Bell Hooks, to honor her maternal great-grandmother. Throughout her life, she championed the significance of writing and critical discourse as tools for challenging and dismantling systems of oppression.

Bell Hooks' work is characterized by its accessibility and its commitment to bridging the gap between academia and the broader public. She believed in making complex feminist and cultural theories accessible to a wider audience, emphasizing the importance of education as a tool for liberation.

One of Hooks' seminal works is "Ain't I a Woman: Black Women and Feminism," published in 1981. In this book, she examined the unique experiences and challenges faced by Black women within the feminist movement and the broader context of American society. Hooks argued that mainstream feminism often failed to fully address the intersectionality of race, class, and gender, and she called for a more inclusive and diverse feminist discourse.

Another influential work by Bell Hooks is "Feminist Theory: From Margin to Center," published in 1984. In this book, she emphasized the need to center the experiences and voices of marginalized groups in feminist theory and activism. Hooks' advocacy for a more inclusive and intersectional feminism has had a profound impact on feminist scholarship and activism.

Hooks continued to explore the intersections of race, class, and gender in her writings, challenging oppressive systems and advocating for social justice. Her work extended to critical analysis of popular culture, including books like "Outlaw Culture: Resisting Representations" and "Black Looks: Race and Representation."

In addition to her written works, Bell Hooks is known for her engaging and thought-provoking lectures and public appearances. She has lectured at universities across the United States, engaging students and the public in discussions about feminism, race, and social justice.

Throughout her career, Hooks remained a steadfast advocate for transformative education and critical thinking. She believed that education had the power to liberate individuals from oppressive systems and that it should empower people to question, analyze, and challenge the status quo.

Bell Hooks' legacy continues to influence feminist thought, critical theory, and discussions on social justice. Her commitment to intersectional feminism and her ability to make complex ideas accessible have left an indelible mark on academia and activism. Her work reminds us of the ongoing importance of acknowledging and addressing the intersecting systems of oppression that affect marginalized communities and the need for inclusive and diverse feminist movements.

Dear Readers,

In celebrating the indomitable spirit of "85 Remarkable Women in History," we invite you to share your thoughts and reflections. Your reviews and insights are guiding lights, helping others navigate the diverse landscape of achievements and contributions within this book.

If these stories resonated with you, if you found inspiration within these pages, or if you believe in the power of honoring pioneers from all walks of life, please consider leaving a review. Your words have the potential to illuminate paths for future generations and ensure that these stories continue to shine brightly.

Thank you for joining us on this transformative journey and for being a part of a community that pays homage to the enduring legacies of extraordinary women.

With heartfelt gratitude, Gabriella Goldberger

Don't miss out!

Visit the website below and you can sign up to receive emails whenever Gabriella Goldberger publishes a new book. There's no charge and no obligation.

https://books2read.com/r/B-A-CNJAB-CUJOC

BOOKS 2 READ

Connecting independent readers to independent writers.

www.ingramcontent.com/pod-product-compliance
Lightning Source LLC
Chambersburg PA
CBHW070519160726
48003CB00004B/1628